ART'S ODYSSEY
— UNPLANNED —

Art Schmitz

Orange Hat Publishing
www.orangehatpublishing.com - Waukesha, WI

Art's Odyssey Unplanned
Copyrighted © 2019 Art Schmitz
ISBN 978-1-64538-036-8
First Edition

Art's Odyssey Unplanned
by Art Schmitz

All Rights Reserved. Written permission must be secured from the publisher to use or reproduce any part of this book, except for brief quotations in critical reviews or articles.

For information, please contact:

Orange Hat Publishing
www.orangehatpublishing.com
Waukesha, WI

Edited by Kaitlyn Hein
Cover design by Kaeley Dunteman

The author has made every effort to ensure that the accuracy of the information within this book was correct at time of publication. The author does not assume and hereby disclaims any liability to any party for any loss, damage, or disruption caused by errors or omissions, whether such errors or omissions result from accident, negligence, or any other cause.

www.orangehatpublishing.com

I dedicate this story to the incredible patience of my wife, Nancy, who had to put up with the lengthy writing process that resulted in this book you're about to read. And to my mother and father, Nora and Art W. Schmitz, and all the others in my life who had to live with, and deal with, the material experienced in this book.

Part 1

I'm writing this story about my early life as the result of questions I've been asked by readers of my book, *A Tourist in Uniform*. My journey through life, at least on my part, was as unplanned at the beginning as was most of the rest of it. As Ma so often put it through the years, "Arthur was born 9 months AND 23 days after we were married." As if anybody else really cared. In other words, my birth didn't have anything to do with my intentions.

I didn't usually have to plan. Somebody else or circumstances did it for me. A few years after I was born, I was faced with the problem of what to do about the new kid in the house. He was a baby boy. Eventually I learned he had a name; Harold. I'd been a fussy eater, so Tante Margaret suggested Ma should make some biscuits, and leave them around the house, and maybe I'd sneakily eat them. It didn't take long for me to find out they made great hard missiles to throw at this little brother who was helpless to do anything about it. Ma and Pa weren't helpless. I had to stand in a corner, and I couldn't have the one thing I would eat, and that was almost any kind of dessert.

When Harold got old enough to know something, he couldn't say my name, but knowing I was a boy, he came up with the name that stuck with me for a long time; Boyce, pronounced Boy-See.

About a year and a half later, another kid showed up, but this time it was totally different. She was a girl. Her name was Eleanore, but we rarely called her that. She became Sis, or as she became older, we'd tease her, calling her baby sister.

I couldn't do enough to keep this kid happy. I'd hold her in my lap. I'd help hold her bottle when that came into the picture.

We lived in an upper flat on North 1st St. Across the alley was a friend of Ma's, and the two women often went to either house for coffee and a gab fest. One cold afternoon, Ma took us kids over to Norma's place.

Sis stayed in the house with the women. Harold and I went to play in the back yard. While we were there, the folks in the lower flat let their two big dogs out in the yard. Harold and I were enjoying a wild frolic with the dogs when Ma came screaming out the door and dragged us back in the house. She thought the dogs were going to kill us.

One warm summer day I was out on the sidewalk in front of the house during a lunch break for some workers doing cement repair work on the street. They'd left a big vat of wet cement on the space between the street and the sidewalk. That turned out to be a revelation for me.

Two kids about my age, a boy and a girl, got naked and stepping into the vat began to cover each other with the wet cement. I'd of course seen Harold naked when we were given baths together, but not Sis. It looked so inviting, I started to take my clothes off when Ma - alerted by somebody - came running out, picking me up with one arm and my clothes with the other, as she hauled me into the house.

We often walked the mile or so to visit Grandpa and Grandma Schmitz, Pa's folks, at 21st and Keefe Avenue. I always enjoyed that visit. One afternoon the three of us were playing in the back yard, but not having much fun in the small yard.

I took Harold and Sis by the hand and began to take them to see Grandma and Grandpa Schmitz, Tante Margaret, and Bobby at their house. Cousin Bobby was almost the same age as I was, but we didn't like each other very much.

We got almost as far as Green Bay Avenue when Ma came running and yelling at us to stop. We did. Marching us in front of her, she made us go in the house still scolding us about getting killed trying to cross Green Bay Avenue. After that, Ma tied me to a clothes line when I was out in the yard.

I had a toy rifle that blew out a small cork when the trigger was pulled, but to do that I had to pull the stock down from just behind the trigger cage, and then push it back up again before firing. I'd done that dozens of times without a problem. But, in a hurry one evening, I got a finger on my right hand squeezed between the stock and the forward part of the gun. Even before that, red had become my favorite color, but I'd never seen any blood before. I took a fascinating look at the blood oozing out of my finger before I started crying, loudly!

We lived in an upper flat near 1st Street and Keefe Avenue before moving out to Granville in 1928. The landlord, who lived downstairs, was a slob to the point that the whole house was infested with everything from cockroaches to moths. The cockroaches were fun to play with. But because of that, the folks decided to move, but not before the whole house was what they called fumigated.

That meant we had to vacate for a few days. I had no idea of what was going on, but enjoying the ride downtown on the 3rd Street streetcar was only a prelude to a greater thrill.

It was little more than a hop, skip, and a jump from the streetcar to boarding an orange coach at the Milwaukee Road train depot. Once on board, we waved to Tante Margaret who'd come down to see us off.

Once the train began to move, I began to try to explore. I'd only taken a few steps from the seat when there was a lurch and I fell to the floor. By the time we reached Madison, I was traversing the entire car with ease.

The only thing I remember about Madison was walking past a fire station near the Lorraine Hotel. The only reason I remember that was because a fire engine there was white, not the red I'd known at home. The folks, their minds on other things, wouldn't believe me when I mentioned it. Not until years later, when we were in Madison and just happened to walk past that same firehouse, was I vindicated.

Not long after that we moved to the northern suburb of Granville. I was 5 years old in our new house when some older neighbor kids asked me to go to the movies with them. With no idea of what a movie was, I was excited at the prospect of getting to experience something new.

Art's Odyssey Unplanned

I went into the house to ask Ma if I could go. Ma's reply was a very definite, "NO!"

I threw a fit, and Ma, trying to explain her reasoning, took me into her lap and completely losing control, I slapped her in the face. I suddenly lost all my anger at the sight of Ma crying. I couldn't say "I'm sorry," but ran into our bedroom.

To me the place was a paradise. There was a sidewalk at the street level, but there was no grass on the terrace or in the back yard, and no concrete walkway from the front porch to the alley behind the house. Plenty of dirt for us to play in.

That made for some interesting circumstances. Tante Margaret wasn't always the nicest person around, but for some reason saw fit to give us kids a set of gardening tools - shovels, rakes, and hoes.

Playing with our new garden stuff at the bottom of the terrace, I decided to take a shovel full of dirt from the other side of the steps. Sis resented my intrusion, and without saying a word, hit me on the head with the hoe she was using. That HURT!

Crying, I ran to the basement window yelling to Ma who was doing the washing down there. Not till I saw my reflection in the cellar window did I realize my face was covered with blood. Ma got me cleaned up, and got our next-door neighbor to drive us to Dr. Doherty's office on Villard Ave.

I didn't remember having been in a doctor's office before, but the strange smells of stuff was overpowering, as was seeing all kinds of shiny paraphernalia in the place. Dr. Doherty washed his hands real good, and started moving hair around on top of my head. It didn't hurt at all.

Then he said, "Now Art, this might sting a little bit but be brave and you'll be okay." He rubbed some stuff on the spot where I'd been hit. It did sting a little, but not enough to make me cry. "Now, Mrs. Schmitz, I didn't have to put any stitches on there, just leave it alone, and Art'll be ok."

Maybe a month or so later, Harold managed to grab the last piece of cake on the table. Sis and I tried to get it away from him as he ran to the back hall, heading for the basement. Tripping on a step, he fell and the plate beat him to the basement floor where his forehead hit pieces of the broken plate, again creating a bloody mess.

We didn't have a phone or a car, so again Ma got our neighbor Mr. Berbaum to drive us to Dr. Doherty's office. This time Dr. Doherty poured some smelly stuff on a piece of cloth, and put it over Harold's nose.

He went to sleep. Except for telling Ma he was going to put some stitches on the cut, nothing else was said. Harold got six stitches, and soon began to wake up again.

We weren't in Granville very long before it became North Milwaukee. Pa walked all day delivering mail, but enjoyed exploring our new area on foot, taking us boys with him on his walks around our house. His reason for not taking Sis was his concern about what to do if she needed a toilet. An appealing destination was the red brick fire house on 35tth Street just south of Villard Avenue, called the village by our neighbors.

The firemen were happy to let Harold and I climb up on the seats of the 2 fire engines in the station.

They even let us hand crank the sirens, just as they did en route to a call. A short time later we became North Milwaukee, and in 1931 the city of Milwaukee, requiring a change of address on the house.

Christmas was THE holiday of the year for us. We usually celebrated at three different locations. We got our presents at home on Christmas Eve, and as often as not, we'd take the bus to Bobby's house for another celebration, and on Christmas Day we'd take the bus and streetcars to Grandma and Grandpa Baker's house on 4th and Lapham on Milwaukee's south side, with another visit to 21st and Keefe in the evening.

After supper there, Harold, Sis, Bobby and I sat in the parlor while the grownups talked at the kitchen table. Not sure why, but I reached out to grab an ornament from the Christmas tree, held it for a minute, and discovered that I'd accidentally squashed it in my hand.

This looked like fun, so Harold, Bobby, and I started to take ornaments from the tree and squash them in our hands. We'd only done a few before Tante Margaret walked in and gave us an earful of words about how terrible we were for ruining all those old and beautiful ornaments.

The Wickman's lived in the house north of us. The older man, a widower who'd come to this country to escape the conscription in his native Sweden, had a job downtown and lived with his single adult daughter, Violet, and her brother Harry with his dog Brownie. Violet worked as a private secretary in an office on the south side, but like many others at the time, Harry didn't have a job. There were many times Harold and

I would talk with Harry and read the pulp magazines he'd give us.

In their house one evening, Harry gave Brownie something to "keep him from getting worms." After we'd asked him what that was, he said "garlic." We'd never heard of it, and Harry told us people ate it too, and used it in cooking.

We were pretty sure nobody we knew was using it, but we asked Harry if we could try some. It was a shock to our systems, but rather than admit that, we asked for some more.

When we woke up the next very cool morning, we asked the folks why all the windows were open. "What did you guys have to eat last night!" Pa asked. Ma wasn't thrilled, but Pa cracked up laughing when we told them about the garlic.

There was some good reading, as far as we were concerned, in those magazines. I especially liked the stories about fighter planes in the World War. The ads too were full of interesting stuff. Everything from booklets about the secrets of various religious groups, and novelty items.

Pa became an unsuspecting victim. I ordered some things that I could put in his cigarettes and when he'd light up, they'd explode. I loaded a whole pack with the things, so Pa soon learned he'd have to wait a little before putting a cigarette to his lips.

Skinny and seeing myself as weak, I didn't think I'd waste any money on the Charles Atlas ads promising to make me into a kind of superman. Besides, it looked like too much work, for an uncertain result.

One winter evening, doing nothing in particular, I felt funny and cried, Pa picked me up and held me over the kitchen sink while I vomited a lot of blood before losing consciousness. I was really totally out of it for a few days, and when I came to, there was a strange lady at my bedside.

I had pneumonia and on the advice of Dr. Doherty the folks had hired a neighbor lady who was a nurse to take care of me. I learned to call her Mrs. Vanoss. She, her husband, and a son younger than I was lived just a few doors down the street.

I hadn't planned on going to school, but at age five one didn't usually question being led off by an older neighbor girl to who knew where. At least I was going somewhere and I loved going to new places; the variety that provided me the spice of life I was looking for.

The pleasure was reinforced when I got to Kindergarten. It was a playground paradise where I was allowed to create huge structures with big blocks light enough for me to lift singlehanded; and a mid-morning snack of milk and graham crackers.

There were vehicles I could ride around the room in, and there were kindly old ladies who took the time to read stories to us and showed us how to march and dance to simple piano tunes.

Going back home for lunch and an afternoon of more play with my own toys in the back yard, or in the house was fun too, except for Harold who wanted to play with the same things I did at the same time. Even at that, life was good. That lasted until I was six years old.

On a cold, cold, raw snow covered day in early February, Ma walked me to the same red brick building that I looked forward to seeing again for more fun and games. I'd vaguely been aware of other rooms in the school, but I wasn't prepared for the shock of being in one of them.

Ma, holding my hand, walked up to a big desk at the front of the room, behind which sat the oldest lady I'd ever seen. There were no playthings of any kind in the room, just rows of chairs connected to desks bolted to the floor.

While Ma and the old lady behind the big desk talked, the old lady had another kid lead me behind the big room where he showed me where to hang my coat, cap, and put my galoshes. When I got back to the room, Ma was gone and the old lady told me where to sit. I was too shocked to cry, but I felt totally deserted and lost.

I was in a sea of strangers but did the only thing I could think of, and that was to try to talk to the kid sitting next to me. I hardly got a "hi kid" out of my mouth when the old lady screamed at me that there was to be NO talking without her permission, whatever that meant, but I got the idea.

The other kid whispered, "She's a bitch," but she didn't hear him, and I was puzzled. I didn't know what a "bitch" was, but I silently agreed with him.

There was no milk and crackers break, but we did get to escape outdoors for 15-minute mid-morning and mid-afternoon recesses. The boys had part of the south, and all of the west side of the playground. The girls had the other part of the south side and all of the east side. After we got in, we went to the boy's lavatory before returning to the room.

I had a problem there. I had to do a number two so went into one of the commodes. The seat was up, but I pushed it down while I got my pants down. I was about to sit down when the seat sprang up and hit my bare butt at the same time as I had my movement. I lucked out when it went where it was supposed to go.

I then had another problem, the toilet paper didn't want to come off the roll fastened to the wall. It took some doing, and it took some time to get all I needed, but eventually my butt was clean and I could escape to the larger prison of the classroom where I was embarrassed when the old lady asked me why it took so long.

We got the daily paper, and there were usually a couple of magazines in the house, so there were plenty of pictures to look at. In the classroom I liked the color pictures of some kids and a dog squeezed in amongst a lot of black markings on the page. I finally found out that the old lady's name was Mrs. Parr, and that she was my teacher.

She talked about stuff she was putting on the blackboard, and I got the idea we were supposed to know what she was talking about. It just looked a lot like the black markings in the book, but with white chalk.

Getting back home after school one day, I heard Eva, the older neighbor girl, tell Ma about hearing Mrs. Parr complaining to Miss McKeatheren, the Principal, that I didn't seem able to do the work. She said that Miss McKeatheren told Mrs. Parr to just fail Arthur and let him take First Grade over again.

The next day Ma took me to school. I went to my seat while Ma and Mrs. Parr chewed the fat at the teacher's desk. From then on, I had homework. Mrs.

Parr had given Ma a lot of paper with big letters and words on them for me to copy.

There were also a lot of papers with parts of words that I had to say for Ma before I could do the things I wanted to do, like go outside and play in the snow with the other kids. The next year I passed into 2nd grade.

I guess I was getting used to the idea that Kindergarten was like the tooth fairy; it wasn't going to happen again. The teacher was Miss Whesker, a lot nicer than old Mrs. Parr, and a lot better looking.

The printed word was beginning to make sense to me too. One Saturday afternoon I was tired, so I crawled under a chifforette and went to sleep. When Ma finally found me, she couldn't wake me up. I was really out of it.

It was fairly late in the evening when I became conscious and vomited. This time Dr. Doherty came to the house. For some weird reason, Ma'd saved my output which Dr. Doherty described as "condensed prune juice."

I had to laugh at that because when someone told Pa something he didn't believe, he said it "sounded like a lot of condensed prune juice." Anyway, it turned out I had pneumonia again, and was out of school till shortly before Christmas. The first couple of times I was able to get out of bed, my legs collapsed under me.

Sick as I had been with pneumonia, I was sick at heart when I got back to school. It didn't dawn on me that I'd missed out on the pre-Christmas stuff in class, and I was really down because I didn't know the words to *Away in a Manger* like the other kids.

The beauty of the melody to me was like music from heaven!

During the art period, we constructed pictures of things of interest to us, using various colored construction paper and paste. Again, the sheer beauty of my creation of a dark sailing ship against a bright golden orange background was a great turn-on for me.

Then came February, and time to pass to the next grade. I had been in 2-B, and it was time to pass to 2-A, but it didn't happen. Nobody had to tell me I'd failed 2-B.

Miss Whesker didn't change my seat. I was still in the same classroom. I was on the verge of tears when she realized my problem. I'd passed to 2-A but it would be in the same room as I'd had for 2-B. That was when Pa introduced me to the opening lines of Hamlet's soliloquy; to be or not to B...

For whatever reason, when I was 8 years old, I refused to eat my breakfast oatmeal. After several minutes of vain attempts to get me to eat it, Pa totally lost it and, taking me over his knee was beating my butt so hard, that besides crying as loud as I could, I had a bowel movement that didn't help the situation. Ma finally threw herself over me and that stopped the beating.

That was about the same time we got a new Principal; a Miss Agnes Murphy. A tall blazing red headed lady, she made her presence felt all over the school. I got to know her quite well; and her secretary, a Miss Benias.

Another year of captivity with the only change of scenery being in Mrs. Schnable's third grade class, across the hall from Miss Whesker's room.

Somewhere along the way, I'd come to enjoy reading, especially the funnies in the Green Sheet, the comic section of our daily afternoon paper.

The Sunday morning paper though was special. All the funnies were in color, and there were comics that didn't appear in the daily paper. I read some of them even if I didn't always understand what was going on, like Dixie Dugan. But I had no problem with Nipper or Napoleon and Uncle Elby, but Tarzan was one of my favorites. I'd read Big Little books with the Tarzan stories, and never missed a Tarzan movie with Johnnie Weismueller.

Sprawled out on the parlor floor I read everything. I especially liked what I called the picture page, although the grownups had a fancier name for it. If it was in the paper, it had to be worth something.

Harold had a cat he called Tubby, an angora. That cat had a knack of laying down right on top of whatever in the paper I was looking at. I had to pick it up and carry it to another room; pushing it off the paper just didn't work, it'd slide right back again.

Until now, I was the only Arthur in a class, but now, there was Arthur Campbell in the seat in front of me. Somehow, we struck each other the wrong way, and began to get physical. He bent down, kicking me under the seat, and it hurt. Reflexively, I hit his back, just below his neck and he yelled out.

Both of us were sent to the Principals office. Miss Murphy read the note from Mrs. Schnabel, wrote a note of her own to Mrs. Schnabel, and sent us back to our room. Mrs. Schnabel ordered us to stay on opposite ends of the cloakroom until lunch, and to stay there during recess as well.

Nothing was said about not talking, so we started out; at first cussing each other out with the few profanities we had learned, gradually moving into asking questions about the other guy's interests and life, and during our recess imprisonment, going to the middle of the cloakroom and shaking hands.

Shortly before lunchtime, Mrs. Schnabel said we could return to the classroom which we did, with our arms around each other's shoulders. We stayed friends until Campbell's dad lost his job and they had to move away.

If anything, Mrs. Schnabel was even more of a bitch than Mrs. Parr. I was having a hell of a time with arithmetic going into multiplication with three numbers at the top and three more at the bottom of a problem, and Mrs. Schnabel didn't seem to be of any help, and I was too scared to ask for any from her.

Miss Murphy wasn't much better. Coming into the building one frigid morning, I had both hands in my pants pockets. Even with gloves on, they'd got cold on the way to school and waiting to be let in the building. She jumped all over me about boys who kept their hands in their pockets were going to wind up in prison!

One fine spring morning when I was 8, Ma took me downtown on the bus and streetcar to see a dentist. It seems my dental situation was in a state of conflict. My baby teeth didn't want to surrender to the onset of my regular teeth coming in. The solution was to put me under with gas, pull the baby teeth, and let nature take its course.

Fascinated by all the gadgetry of the place, the dentist explained he was going to put this mask over my face that would put me to sleep while he pulled the teeth. I wouldn't feel a thing, and when I woke up, I'd be just fine.

I didn't know how long it took, but I felt great and ready to go home. He'd pulled 8 teeth. The dentist told us I could have soup and very soft food, and that I should not do anything very active for the rest of the day. Money was tight I knew, but I felt like a king riding home in a Checker Cab instead of the cheaper Yellow Cab, or a slow and pokey streetcar.

Once home, Ma fixed me a bowl of chicken soup with a butter bread sandwich and a glass of milk. Right after lunch Ma had a migraine, took some aspirin, and laid down on the davenport in the parlor. A few minutes later, Harold and I heard the familiar sound of sirens, chasing out of the house to assist in yet another of the grass fires on Hopkins Street.

I was 9 when my cousin Kenny gave Harold a toy boat he'd made. I was really ticked that he'd given the boat to Harold instead of me, so I headed down to the basement to even things out. I'd show them! I'd make my own boat.

Finding a small piece of wood about the same size as the boat Kenny'd made, I began to work on it. First I had to take the more or less rectangular piece of wood and shape it. Before I could do anything with it, Kenny, looking through the open basement window asked, "What're you doing, Boyce?" I yelled back, "I'm gonna make my own boat."

We didn't have a lot of tools, including a vise to hold anything, so holding the wood in my left hand, I

Art's Odyssey Unplanned

brought down the small hatchet to slice off a diagonal piece to shape the bow of my boat. That was as far as I got. Somehow or other, the hatchet found its way to the index finger of my left hand, leaving the wood intact.

It hurt like blazes and bled a lot, but I didn't dare cry out loud and let everyone in the house know I'd messed up. With a quick shove of my wounded finger into my mouth so nobody'd see the blood, I kept holding my left arm up and eventually it stopped bleeding, but didn't stop hurting.

I couldn't put a bandage on my wound because Ma'd want to know what happened.

So, whenever I was with the others I kept my left hand in my pants pocket. It didn't look real good when I'd look at it, kind of a mix of blueish purple and green, but the pain subsided and after a few days it looked and felt better, and best of all, nobody else ever knew what happened.

Finally escaping from Mrs. Schnabel, I passed into 4-B, with Mrs. Kohl in charge.

One side of the room was 4-B, and the other side was 4-A, the next level up. Although I was, as usual, having real problems with long division, my eyes and ears were tuned to what was going on at the other side of the room.

From day one, I wasn't crazy about doing the written work the teachers wanted, and I never mastered the fine art of using what they called arm-movement or, as the cover of the handwriting booklet said, "The Palmer Method" when writing, so a lot of the written class work just didn't get done. I did get to pass to 4-A.

After a parent-teacher evening, the folks told the family about an impression I'd made on Mrs. Kohl. We'd been studying about Indians and Mrs. Kohl asked us why we thought the Indians had such steady nerves when it came to accurately shooting their bows and arrows at a target. My answer was, as I'd read in the funnies, "Because they smoked Camels cigarettes." To me, whatever was in the newspaper had to be true.

I was scared stiff of thunder storms. Sitting on the front porch with Pa on a summer evening, I jumped every time I heard the thunder after a flash of lightning. Asking Pa what caused the thunder, he gave me the answer. "You're hearing the sound of the angels bowling in heaven." Then he added, "It's not the thunder you have to worry about. When you hear the thunder, you know it's all right," adding that it's the lightning that can hurt you.

As time went on, I often stayed at Bobby's house. Although we still didn't like each other very much, I loved the sound of the chimes of the old clock they had, and Grandma Schmitz let me, but none of the other kids, play records on her Victrola.

At 9 years old, I was alone in the upper flat with Grandma Schmitz. Bobby was out with some of his friends. Grandma, taking my hand, took me outside and we walked down Keefe Avenue to the Egyptian Theater on Teutonia Avenue.

As we walked, she told me how she loved going to the movies, but couldn't take Bobby. She'd tried it once, but he screamed when they were seated in the dark theater.

Going in, I was captivated by the setting. Sure,

the place was dark, but the side walls were softly illuminated with weird masks and statues, and the ceiling was as a starlit night in contrast to the bright sunlight outside.

When the curtains parted and the show began, I was enthralled with the action on screen. The previews of coming shows, short subjects, and cartoons were all one and the same magic. There was a breathtaking scene of Harold Lloyd high above the ground hanging on a clocks hands, Grandma squeezing my hand as tight as she could.

I don't know if she knew what the coming movies were going to be, but I began to sense she had some misgivings about taking me to see *Scarface*, a crime film.

She wouldn't take no for an answer when she suddenly pulled me out of my seat before I completely lost my innocence. The cause was a cartoon showing a line of ducks crapping as they waddled along. I thought it was hilarious!

About the same time, on weekends, the relation would gather for a picnic at a park; often at McKinley or South Shore Beach. Pa would take Harold and I to the bath house to change into our swimming suits.

We came off as the midgety "paleskins" - we'd heard that the Indians called us that compared to the huge hunks of the hairy older guys' bodies. We never gave it a thought that we were seeing ourselves some years ahead. That, and the uninhibited profane and obscene language we heard in the adult banter, was also something we never thought we'd be doing any time in the future.

One of the differences between Bobby and I was

that I was a pathological reader, and he was almost the direct opposite. Where Tante Margaret got them, I don't know, but there was always a big supply of reading material for kids that were imports from England.

Not only did they introduce me to the linguistic differences between British English and ours, but they were really funny and interesting reading. I don't know if they were English or not, but I enjoyed reading the stories about Billy Goat Gruff.

As I grew older, there were many times when I'd be alone in the house with Grandma, especially after Grandpa died. She'd tell me about being a kid in Prussia, and tossing a bouquet to the Crown Prince when a parade marched past their home, and he'd blown her a kiss. Often, as she'd talk, she'd lapse into German that I gradually began to understand.

She'd been something of a favorite with her father. Even though he knew she'd be up in a tree reading, he'd pretend ignorance of her whereabouts if other family members wanted her to help with something.

After that, movies were a regular part of life, not just for me, but for Sis and Harold as well; especially Saturday matinees at the Ritz Theater on Villard Avenue.

I guess it's true that we never really forget anything. As a GI home on furlough during World War II, I went back to my old grade school; most of my teachers were still there, including Mrs. Kohl, my 4-A teacher.

The school day was over, and as we talked, she reminded me of an episode I'd totally forgotten about. It took place on a warm spring day. Without a prior thought, I'd got out of my front seat, walked down the row, and bent down to kiss Maria Bentley's knee. Nobody, Mrs. Kohl included, said or did anything as I returned to my front seat. Maria was wearing a bright yellow dress that day and to me, for the moment at least, was irresistible.

One day, toward the end of the semester in 4th grade, Miss Murphy took me out of the room and led me to a small room with a table and chair, explaining that I was to take a special test. I wouldn't be disturbed, but if I had any questions I could ask her. The test took a long time, but I was intrigued by the questions, most of which were easy to answer.

A week later, I knew I was in big trouble when Miss Murphy asked both Ma and Pa to come with me for a conference in her office. I knew that Ma and Pa were worried too.

After shuffling some papers around on her desk, Miss Murphy came right to the point. "I'm so glad both of you were able to come here today. As you know, Arthur was tested last week, and there's where we have the problem."

"Because of the obvious problems Arthur seems to be having with his schoolwork, we decided to give him the test to see exactly how intelligent he is. However, Arthur, I think it will be better if you go back to your class now."

Not really knowing what Miss Murphy was talking about, I was more than happy to escape her office, but took my time, including a stop at the boy's room before going back to the class.

At home that evening, Ma and Pa explained the situation. They knew I was going to be tested, but hadn't said anything because they thought I'd flunk it on purpose.

If I failed the test, I would have been sent to a special class at the Clarke St. School, and would have had to take the bus and streetcar to get there. I would have been thrilled to have to do that!

It turned out that the problem Miss Murphy was talking about was that I'd got the highest score of any previous pupil who'd taken the test at that school, so I'd continue as before at the same school. It seems the problem was that my schoolwork didn't reflect the knowledge and learning that was taking place in my mind. The grownups were more worried about that than I was.

I quit. No, I don't mean that I'm quitting this travelogue of life. I've just finished reading Mark Twain's autobiography, and the way he wrote it makes sense - to me at least. Instead of writing it in strict chronological order, he dictated it to his secretary as ideas and memories occurred to him, and that's what I'm gonna do here from now on.

I must've been about 12 years old when Pa took me along to have some work done on the '33 Plymouth sedan he was driving. Sitting on a work bench at the rear of the shop while he and the mechanic talked, I whiled away the time by swinging my legs back and forth between the empty space below the bench and outward.

As I swung, my legs gained momentum and with no warning my upper body swung out away from the bench and my legs dropped into a large container below the bench. As I swung out away from the bench, the container spilled its strong, smelly contents on the floor about the same time I landed belly down on the floor.

Pa simply said, "Just sit down on the floor until we're ready to go." The mechanic added, "Don't worry, that's just distillate. Except for being a stinky mess, it won't hurt you any."

Before driving home, Pa and his friend filled the back seat of the car with as many newspapers as they could find. The tough part came when we got home. I had to strip completely down in the basement, and using clean rags and hot water from the wash tubs, clean my body of the distillate residue. Then, afraid I might not have gotten it all, I had to come upstairs, naked, then take a tub bath just to make sure.

This wasn't the first time I had to get rid of my clothes in the basement. A few years before, Harold and I wound up down there because we made the mistake of trying to relive history in our bedroom.

Ma was having one of her migraine headaches which some of her relatives blamed on us. We didn't have school that day, and the weather outside was frightful, so we obeyed as Ma'd ordered us to play quietly in our bedroom.

Between reading about history and geography, and hooked on radio programs such as *March of Time* and *Cavalcade of America*, we decided, with the aid of our toy soldiers, to reenact the encampment of Valley Forge. To create the proper conditions, of course, required something to replicate the snowy conditions that Washington's troops endured.

A common item in our house was a can of white stearate zinc powder, augmented with a generous scattering of white flour over our troops and almost everything else in the room that satisfied our creative impulse. That is, until late in the afternoon when Ma woke up and took in the situation!

I think you could have heard her six blocks away! She shagged us downstairs to get out of our "simulated snowy" clothes. In the comparative safety of the cellar we took our time, while her tirade continued upstairs. Pa, coming home from work, came in the back door, and realizing almost instantly that Harold and I were in the basement, came down, saying "What's the matter guys, the artillery go off upstairs?"

Harold and I couldn't wait for weekends. Although Pa had to work Saturday mornings, he was home for afternoons. It was one of those warm, balmy May days when Harold and I, for no special reason, were walking past old man Wohlfahr's place with our coaster wagon, a couple of blocks from home. He was a gruff, intimidating guy to us kids, but he and Pa got along well.

With his strong German accent, he yelled at us, "Boyss, come'll hier," adding, "I haf somzings fur yur Papa!" We waited on the sidewalk while he loaded our wagon with several bottles of homebrew. "Now," he ordered, "Take zat home right avay. Macht schnell!"

We got as far as the corner, when a half block away we saw the first of a couple of fire engines heading south on Hopkins Street. Instead of turning right to get the homebrew to our place, the 6th house north, we headed hell-bent for election to Hopkins Street, and several blocks south where as interested spectators, we helped the firemen douse a stubborn grass fire.

Mission accomplished, we headed home, where the others were already at the table for lunch. Joining them, Harold and I told the family about the grass fire. During a lull in the conversation, Harold mentioned the homebrew sitting in the wagon on the sidewalk in front of the house.

I don't know who was happier to get some beer, Pa or Grandma Baker, who was living with us. Pa ran out and put the beer on the table. Immediately after he opened the first bottle, Harold and I ran out the back door as Ma screamed at the sight of fountains of homebrew hitting the ceiling.

If Pa being home Saturday afternoons was great, Sundays were sensational. We didn't have a car, but on Sunday – with a one dollar bus and streetcar pass, an adult could ride, along with 2 kids under 12 all day long anywhere in the city.

Usually, it'd be Pa, Harold, and our cousin Bobby who had a lot of fears. My only fear was getting beat up by the bullies at school, but Bobby was afraid of his own shadow. A couple of other older cousins would tell us about the great travel lectures offered on weekends at the Museum, but nobody under 12 could attend. I was miffed.

I don't know if they just weren't interested or what, but neither Harold or Sis ever seemed to go with Ma or our cousin Dorothy to church on Sunday mornings, but they'd usually take me. Ma and most of her relatives belonged to *Die Neue Apostoliche Kirche* on 4th and Wright.

I reveled in the streetcar ride, but without understanding most of the sermon or hymns, which were all in German, I enjoyed the dramatic bombast of the preachers and the out-of-this world melodies which were sung a capella.

One Sunday afternoon, after getting off Streetcar #15, and then walking from Kinnickinnick, Pa took us to the Grand Trunk car ferry docks. I guess it was because this was at the height of the Great Depression, but there wasn't much doing there at the time.

A man on board yelled down asking us if we'd like to come on board. Harold and I were thrilled to be actually boarding this, the largest thing on the water that we'd ever seen. Bobby almost cried with the fear that it would sail with us on board, with Harold and I seeing that remote possibility as relieving us from school.

We toured the boat from the bridge to the lowest levels of the engine room, asking our poor, but patient host umpteen questions. I don't know if that was a factor, but both Harold and I had our eyes on the Navy later on. When we finally left the car ferry, a little dirtier but happy; even Bobby felt good.

I was about nine when the stamp collecting bug hit me. There was a radio program sponsored by Ivory Soap, featuring a Captain Tim Healy, who with a smoothly suave voice, and a hint of an aristocratic English accent, related exciting stories about the postage stamps of the world.

Pa working as a mailman helped. When delivering a letter with a foreign stamp, he wasn't allowed to ask for it. But there was nothing that said he couldn't tell the recipient that his son was a stamp collector, and as often as not, they'd give him the whole envelope.

Captain Healy's stories were of high adventure

and mysterious skullduggery - featuring places and people featured on the stamps. For a small amount of change and an Ivory Soap wrapper sent in, one received a paperback stamp album.

Times were tough, and money scarce, so anything we could do for free, we did. The museum was one of those places we visited often, and almost always saw something new.

One of the standbys for me was a huge stamp collection mounted in vertical pull out frames. Some famous, rich Milwaukee guy had donated his collection to the museum. I never tired of looking at it.

Another totally different kind of collection donated to the museum was the butterfly collection, also neatly mounted and properly labeled with the scientific Latin names of the specimens. That exhibit was responsible for providing me with hours of active fun.

I managed to fix myself a net to catch butterflies, and often moths that looked like butterflies. I learned how to kill both species and the differentiating features between them, and mount the butterflies in cigar boxes that served as proper storage places. I hoped that one day I could have a display like the one at the museum.

Ma, with her phobia about moths, was anything but encouraging. I tried to show her the differences between butterflies and moths, but as long as it had the same kind of wings, it was a moth.

I don't know where the violin came from, but when I was nine, we learned I could get group violin lessons once a week for a semester for $2. The lessons were given at Custer High School after school.

Art Schmitz

I didn't understand the directions the teacher gave us, and was too dumb to know how to ask for an explanation. I went through the motions, but didn't learn much more than how to use the resin on the bow.

There was a fun element involved. Our group got its lesson on the stage of the auditorium. While waiting for our lesson to begin, some of us would explore our surroundings, including climbing up a winding stairway at the side of the stage, and checking out the various ropes and metal elements involved in managing curtain operations as we carefully walked across cat walks from one side of the stage to the other, and back.

Pa, after a series of discussions lasting over a fairly long period, finally said that when I was twelve, I could go solo on Sunday with a streetcar pass. And, when that happy twelfth birthday came, it was just the precursor to the freedom of the first Sunday after it.

Traveling alone with the pass wasn't quite enough traveling for me. I had a destination in mind. I didn't know what was on the program, but I was definitely going to exercise the privileges of being twelve by going to the travel lecture at the Museum.

The folks had often taken us kids to the exhibits at the Museum, but the lecture hall was new territory for me. The lecture began at 3:30 p.m., but I was there well before that.

Awestruck by just being there, I made certain I had a seat well away from the huge wrought iron framework of the lights suspended above the auditorium. Scanning the audience of old people, I quickly realized the huge satisfaction of being the only kid in the place.

The lecturer walked out on the stage, the lights went out, and his travelogue began with black and white movies. It soon became obvious that it was far more educational than anything I'd learned in school.

Sure, I was learning about how explorers could bring back the clean skeleton of a large Amazonian animal by immersing the dead body into a fury of piranhas.

But the real item was my exposure to the natives of all ages, and both genders minus any clothing at all. Learning that the same lecture had been given on the previous Friday evening, and twice the day before, I realized I could have enjoyed the lecture multiple times if I'd known about it.

The lecture ended around 5:30, and I suddenly knew there was no way I'd be home in time for supper at 6. Ma was a real worry-wart, so with a nickel out of my weekly allowance of a quarter, I slowly, to make sure I didn't make any mistake that'd cost me anything, made my first phone call from a pay phone.

Once in the clear about not having a set time to get home, I walked over to a White Tower restaurant, and for 10 cents, had a hamburger and a cup of coffee before boarding the #12 streetcar.

At the bus station on 27th and Hopkins, I spent another dime for a cruller and coffee before getting on the #59 bus to home. Ma'd kept some supper ready for me, including strawberry shortcake for dessert.

Almost every weekend found me at one, or more,

of the free lectures at the museum. I was also taking in every movie I could afford to see; sometimes getting lucky enough to have the folks take me along if they went.

About the same time, I was reading everything in either the school or public library that looked interesting, exciting, and/or adventurous. It was coincidence that I found books by Commander Ellsberg almost simultaneously with movies of his stories about Naval Diving and submarine rescues. This was for me.

Not being the well-coordinated kid where sports were concerned, I was ripe for something I thought I could do for the thrills and adventures my peers got from sports. The answer was obvious - I'd make my own diving helmet.

Finding an empty square metal container, measuring about a foot wide and a bit longer from top to bottom, I had the basic equipment. I managed to cut a small space out of one side of it for what became a window; I got the local hardware store to cut me a piece of glass to fit it, and cut rounded spaces out of each side to fit over my shoulders. Nobody asked me what I was doing - I don't think anyone cared.

Cutting a small hole in the metal top, I managed to insert the air valve from an old inner tube to connect to about 20 feet of rubber tubing. My buddy, Kenny Isaacson and I, carrying my diving helmet walked the mile or so to the Milwaukee River where we were able to talk a guy into letting us use his small boat to try out my diving helmet.

Stripping to our trunks, I put the helmet over

my head, easing my arms through some wash line fastened to each end of the shoulder spaces, while Ken hooked the tubing to a tire pump we'd brought along, and I slipped over the side of the boat in about ten feet of water. Ken began pumping, but I had to push myself against the bottom of the boat to get below the surface of the river. My feet and legs wanted to come up, but I was able to breathe and there was enough pressure to keep water below my chin.

Getting an affirmative when we asked the boat's owner if we could use his boat again, we got dressed and headed home. A couple of days later we were back for trial 2. This time, with a brick tied to each foot, we had the buoyancy problem licked, but we got lucky with using the tubing to help me get back to the surface. At home I punched a very small hole in one side near the top to allow excess air to escape.

The river had one great advantage. The water was much warmer than any of the lakes in our neck of the woods. The next day we were back, this time with at least 30 feet of wash line tied around my waist to solve the return trip to the surface problem. Finally, I actually got to the bottom of the river.

I'd been hoping to see some forms of freshwater marine life. I'd fished the area often enough to know there was a variety of fish in the vicinity, but no such luck.

I could hardly see my hand in front of my face; the water was so murky to start with, and the added clouds of mucky bottom stirred up by my feet didn't help, but it felt really great to be completely submerged in the warm wetness of the river.

Giving a yank on the wash line, Ken helped pull

me up. Disappointed at not being able to see much, we headed for home, but thrilled with the fact that our adventure had been a success. Time marched on, and there were other things to captivate my interest, but water remained a big part of that.

Then came the moment of truth. Actually going into Lake Michigan in swimming suits covering our entire bodies, from just above the knees to our shoulders. We screamed as our crotches met the icy cold water of the lake for the first time.

We weren't going to let that stop us from getting to enjoy the obvious fun everyone else seemed to be having on this really hot day. We tried to imitate the movements of others who were swimming, but wound up getting a face full of funny tasting water down our nose and into our mouths. But, it was a start.

Not too much later, Ma'd give us a nickel a piece, and Harold, Sis, and I'd head to Silver Spring Park where for that nickel we could get swimming lessons in the morning. It didn't work for me. I went through the motions, but never seemed to get my arms and legs to work together to let me move through the water like everyone else.

Later that summer, sitting on the edge of the pool at the 14-foot level, I was enjoying the freedom of being there, and the shades of color of the water from one depth to another when Ray Bastian, a friend of our bunch, pushed me off the edge and into the water.

For once in my life, I kept my mouth shut, and my eyes open. I was too mad to be scared. I'll fix that bastard, I thought. I let myself drop to the bottom, and still marveling at the beauty of the water, I started to

Art's Odyssey Unplanned

crawl toward shallower water when I realized I could, with my arms and legs move myself under water. I was SWIMMING!

By that time, I was at the 9-foot level, and rising to the surface, quietly grabbed onto a drainage edge, and pulled myself up to sit on the pool edge and watch. I was chortling while watching Ray straining his eyes trying to see where I was, obviously worried at not finding me, while walking back and forth along the area.

Not until I saw him approach the life guard did I stand up, waving, and yelling "over here!" He ran over, despite signs saying, "NO RUNNING." When he got to me, I stepped back as he gave me a bear hug, saying "You son-of-a bitch, you had us scared stiff!" when I gave him a shove sending him flying backwards into the water. "Now we're even." I yelled, and walked away thrilled knowing that now I could swim.

As time progressed, Harold, Sis, Bobby, and I'd head for Silver Spring Park a couple of times a week. When we got to where the railroad tracks crossed Hopkins St., we'd take the substantial short cut along the tracks that passed the edge of the park. I knew there were only two passenger trains a day; one in the morning, and another in the evening, and occasionally a slow freight. So getting hit by a train wasn't a concern, but Bobby'd always take the much longer walk up Hopkins St. to Silver Spring Road and west to the park.

Maybe it was the intense heat and high humidity, but while we didn't actually come to blows, we were always involved in intense arguments about anything we could think of, that we knew someone would disagree with.

By the time I was 12, most of my friends had bikes. Pa'd had some kind of bad experience when he was a kid, so any mention of a bike was met with "Over my dead body." But, in a weak moment I got him to say, "when you can pay for it yourself", and I'm dead sure he never figured that would happen; not with a quarter a week allowance, an extra 50 cents a week from delivering an advertising circular, and the occasional quarter for babysitting a kid down the street.

But, to help make ends meet, the folks rented a room to a young couple. Bill was a used car salesman. He'd pay Harold and I to spot other agencies, copying down license plates of cars being looked at by sales people. Bill would use the numbers to find out who they belonged to, make the contact, and often make a sale. The work was easy, we got to go places like downtown on our own, and got out of whatever jobs Ma or Grandma wanted us to do. We started to make money in the form of actual dollars.

The day finally came when I saw a Schwinn bicycle on sale at Schuster's for $32. I had the money, but Pa was still stubborn. "If you can find a way of getting it home, fine." In other words, we had a car, but he wasn't going to use it for this.

Luckily, we had a neighbor who was in the automotive department at the 12th Street Schuster's store. Paying my own fare, I took the streetcar to the store, gave Ed the money, and he brought the bike home in his car after work. I had my bike!

We had a few dollars left over, but even at that, it

was almost a year before we had enough to get Harold his bike. This time Pa drove to get it for us. My bike was a red and cream, and Harold's was a black and cream. Summer and winter, the bikes stood on the upper front lawn when not in use. For some weird reason, the space between the bikes became the repository for our cats hunting success during the night; mice, birds, and sometimes a big old rat.

The first Halloween after Harold had his bike, he, Gropp, and I were riding the neighborhood streets with nothing particular in mind. As we passed parked cars, we found that by flipping the antennas on the fenders, we could get a nice twanging sound when they bounced back.

We'd been doing that for a while when I suddenly found I was riding with an antenna in the fist of my right hand. I dropped it on the road at the end of the block, and we hightailed away from there as fast as we could. We didn't do any more antennas.

I always got a kick out of the evening before Halloween. We called it Tick Tock night. We'd take a wooden sewing spool minus the thread, notch the edges, tie a string around the thick part of the spool, and go to houses where we could see people at home.

Sticking a pencil through the hole of the spool, we'd press the spool against the glass of a door or window; pull hard on the string, causing the spool to rotate and make a terrible noise as if the glass was breaking. Then we'd run like mad away from that house and head for the next target, as porch lights would come on.

Walking to school a few days before Halloween, I heard a couple of girls walking in front of me talking about the Halloween party they were planning. It was only when they mentioned our family name that I bothered paying any attention to the details they were discussing.

"We should invite the Schmitz kids 'cause their mother always bakes a cake for parties like this." I almost felt like telling them where they could shove their party, but I didn't. Harold, Sis and I all went, with the cake Ma made, and we had a great time doing everything from bobbing apples to eating popcorn balls and eating Ma's cake.

Shortly after my streetcar pass emancipation, I was reading a book one evening that had a Boy Scout adventure story. We often heard Pa criticizing the scouts as a way of enticing boys into the army when they got old enough. As proof, he cited the fact that their uniforms were the same color, OD, as the army's, and even their hats were the same.

I was really surprised when, after a visit to our neighborhood library, I told Pa I'd like to go to the next local Boy Scout meeting, and he said he'd like to go along! A week or so later, we walked over to the Carleton School on Silver Spring road for the meeting of Troop 5, Boy Scouts of America. He even paid the nominal membership fee for me.

Being the klotz I was with manual dexterity, mastering the intricacies of tying the various knots required to become a Tenderfoot, was a real challenge for me.

Eventually I made it, and after that I even got my 2nd Class award, but never made it past that point. Not that I tried that hard, I was just enjoying the camaraderie of the troop, new friends, and the

Art's Odyssey Unplanned

various hiking and camping excursions involved.

Before we got our bikes, Harold and I, even when we weren't able to ride buses and streetcars, got around town. Kenny Isaacson had a cousin living way over on the east end of the North Avenue viaduct. Somehow or other the three of us managed to beg or borrow roller skates, that we used to skate all the way across town to see Ken's cousin. It took us most of a Saturday morning to get there, before having lunch with Ken's aunt, his cousin, visiting, and getting home in time for supper.

Now, with bikes to spread our wings, we spent the first available Saturday with a ride out to Greenfield Park, way hell-and-gone to the southwest corner of the county. Not really knowing how to get there, we didn't bother to tell anyone else, like parents, of our destination.

Our reason for Greenfield Park as a destination was that it was the newest park in the Milwaukee County Park System, supposedly with swimming pool features missing at the other parks. The fact that the swimming pool season hadn't opened yet was a meaningless element in our plans. The knowledge that it was a 16-mile ride one way, wasn't known to us, didn't preclude an interesting excursion.

We knew in a general way where the park was, meaning we sort of explored our route across the city, dodging busy traffic, streetcar tracks, and strange looks from passersby's to get there. We had a blast!

Looking over the closed pool, not yet filled with water, we headed for home. We hadn't expected our ride there and back to take that long, so we missed having lunch but did get home in time for supper.

Unusually early for a Saturday evening, Harold and I hit the sack right after supper. We managed to get up for breakfast Sunday morning, but went back to bed instead of going to Sunday school or church.

By Monday morning it was clear that we were both sick. It wasn't till then that Ma started giving us an earful about overdoing things when we should've known better, etc., etc., etc., and on, and on.

We didn't mind missing school for a couple of days. Figuring we'd get better with some rest, we pretty much ignored the harangue with ideas of other faraway places beckoning to us.

We learned that Ken was in the same boat. The one change in our thinking being that, never again would we go anywhere without some provision for lunch or any other meal we might otherwise miss.

Pa's first car was a used four-door blue box on wheels; a 1927 Essex he got for $25 in 1932. We loved going for joy rides, windows open, and making siren noises whenever he got it to go over 35 miles an hour. At least half the time he had to really crank it to start the engine.

Whenever we bounced across a railroad track, we'd burst into song, singing "A peanut sat on a railroad track, it's heart was all aflutter. The Limited came 'round the bend, toot, toot, peanut butter!"

Once we had a car, Pa'd take us to places not too easily reached by bus or streetcar. One of my favorite spots was the playground at Estabrook park. It had swings unlike any others I'd ever seen. We wound up going there fairly often.

A few years before that, Hans, the boyfriend of a woman Ma'd grown up with, was our chauffeur one

Art's Odyssey Unplanned

Sunday afternoon. Ma's sister Tante Minnie and her husband were trying to make it on a farm out in the country. Caring nothing for the dull gabbing the grownups were doing, us kids sat in Hans's car, me at the wheel, pretending we were going places.

There were a couple of silvery levers near the steering wheel that I'd seen Hans use on the way out, so I moved them as far as they'd go and back again. We piled out of the car, and ran into the parlor where the folks were talking, when smoke started coming out of the steering wheel. We heard something about "magneto" and "battery" as Hans ran out to his car, muttering bad words to himself. We rode home with a friend of Uncle Paul's.

Grandpa Schmitz was an old man when he died in 1932. He'd been blind for years because he had diabetes. The day of his funeral, the grownups - without telling us - went for lunch, leaving Bobby, Harold, Sis and I alone at the funeral parlor with Grandpa's body.

In front and to one side of the casket was a stand with a light and papers on it. With the stand in front of me, and the other three kids sitting in chairs, I started making a speech.

Very serious, at least at the beginning, I began to ad lib with stuff like "Friends, Romans, and countrymen..." going on to add stuff I knew would make the other kids laugh. That was about the time the grownups got back from lunch. Grandma Schmitz screamed hysterically, but at least we weren't alone anymore.

Things went downhill from there. Nobody'd told us kids about the formalities of a Masonic funeral.

During the proceedings, a group of somber faced men marched down the aisle toward the casket. Harold, Bobby, and I took one look, and couldn't restrain ourselves from suppressing giggles to outright laughing out loud. The serious faces under the tall hats and above the aprons they wore made it seem to us as if they were a group of butchers marching in. To Grandma Schmitz, we became persona non grata to the nth degree.

Our second car was a '32 Plymouth 4 door sedan with something called Free Wheeling, and could go a lot faster than the old Essex's 35 miles an hour. Our first overnight trip was to Lacrosse where Pa had a friend, and because Pa wanted to see the Mississippi River.

After a very brief visit with Pa's friend, we drove to a place on the banks of the river. Harold and I moaned the blues about not having any fishing stuff with us. After having supper at a small restaurant, Pa parked on a side street near a busy square, and we tried to settle down to sleep the night away.

It was hot and muggy, and we could hear the blare of an orchestra at a dance hall across the street most of the night. Ma'd packed some cereal and breakfast dishes, but being Sunday we couldn't find a store open for milk, so we had another (better) breakfast at a restaurant, before heading east towards home.

Pa detoured toward the zoo at Vilas Park in Madison, but cut that short when Ma developed a migraine. Besides, it was just too darned hot to be able to enjoy much of anything so we headed for the relative comforts of home.

Later that summer we headed east, this time

Art's Odyssey Unplanned

aiming for Niagara Falls. With a borrowed tent, one of our first stops was at a private camp ground outside of Battle Creek, Michigan.

We toured the Kellogg Cereal Company plant, coming out with enough sample 8 packs to take care of breakfast for the rest of our trip. Ma gloated for the rest of the trip about being able to debunk her mother's ideas about how breakfast cereal was produced.

During some free time, I got to know a girl my age at the camp. Besides being good looking, she was a lot of fun. She dared me to touch the Ohio license plate on her Dad's car. I couldn't see that as a problem. The next thing I knew I was knocked flat on my butt! The electric shock of the wired license plate didn't hurt, but boy was I surprised. I couldn't help laughing with her. She was really cute!

Grandpa Schmitz was born in Germany, but at 14 ran away from home, joined the English navy, and jumped ship in this country some years later. That had a bearing on how we sometimes reacted to his wishes.

For whatever reason, Grandma Schmitz trusted me to handle her records and the old windup Victrola. Occasionally Grandpa'd ask me to play "Bummel Petrus," Lazy Peter, an old German folk tune.

Often, instead of acceding to his request, I'd put something like Wayne King's "A Window in a House in Caroline" on the Victrola; especially if Bobby and Harold were around.

That's when Grandpa's frustration at his visual limits found an outlet, much to our satisfaction as he'd let fly with all the profane obscenities of his former naval days - after which we could impress our peers on the playground at school. Not that we understood half of what we'd heard.

Shortly after my 10th birthday, Pa had a day off. He got Harold and I up so early it was still dark outside. He didn't break our hearts when he told us he was going to keep us out of school for the day.

Right after breakfast, we left the house, got on the #59 bus, transferred to a #12 streetcar and headed downtown. Not until we'd boarded the North Shore Electric train did we know we were going to Chicago!

While staying overnight at Grandma Baker's little tar paper shack, we'd spend hours sitting on the church steps at 6th and Mitchell Street watching the North Shore electric trains heading south to Chicago. Now we were among the royalty able to enjoy riding high above city streets without stopping to pick up other less privileged passengers.

Although it was over a two hour ride, it seemed like no time at all before we were riding high above the busy traffic of Chicago's streets on the elevated tracks. By this time, Pa'd told us we were going to the 1933 World's Fair.

Walking from the L station we reached the grounds of the World's Fair. Harold and I got light weight fireman's hats at the Texaco exhibit, pin on pickles from Heinz, and toy dinosaurs from Sinclair gasoline.

We were awestruck at seeing tires vulcanized at Firestone, and enthralled by being able to walk through railway coaches and locomotives represented by rail companies we'd never heard of before. We ate a cheap lunch at the Chinese governments booth, and

Art's Odyssey Unplanned

marveled at an intricately designed and operating miniature village before riding the Skyway from the main area to the adjacent island.

Each of the gondolas was named for a character on the *Amos and Andy* radio program. With a vague idea that it sounded bad, we looked forward to shocking adults and impressing our peers because we got into Ruby Taylor.

It was long past our usual nine o'clock bedtime when we walked back to the L station for the return trip home. We'd never seen after hours entrances to stores closed and protected by steel gates. We wondered why Chicago fire engines, besides the usual red lights, displayed red and green lights as they sped to an alarm.

Reaching the L platform, a drunk approached Pa saying, "Youse guys are from Milwaukee, ain'tcha?" Pa said, "Yeah, but how did you know?" The guy said, "Shimple, I could shee da sauerkraut hangin' outa yer ears!" Harold and I cracked up imagining what that would look like.

We were still revved up after what was the most exciting day of our lives, and told Pa as much, bragging we were going to stay awake all the way home. Pa agreed, saying "You guys'll be out before we get to Evanston." We strenuously argued the point, but he was right.

Usually in spring, with Bobby along, Pa'd take us by bus and streetcar to Soldiers Home. As usual, he didn't say where we were going, but after getting off the streetcar we knew.

Walking across fields of grass, we could hear the stirring sounds of bugles and the base beats of drums in the distance. It was the annual competition of Drum and Bugle Corps of the various veteran's groups.

We'd stand aside and watch them marching and changing formations as they played soul stirring music we could feel. The uniforms varied from fairly simple military like hats, jackets, and pants to bright blue tunics, white pants, and shiny silvery helmets.

The entire facility was open to the public. Pa led us through different sections of the hospital where we saw firsthand men still suffering from the mental problems and gas impacted effects of the war.

There was another fun side of the day. Free full length movies were shown in the theater. One especially intrigued us. It was Wallace Beery in *West of the Pecos*. A wagon train, when attacked by Indians, formed a defensive circle. Each time Wallace Beery fired a shot, he took a swig from his bottle. The effect of his drinking made for an interesting doubling of his victims count after each shot. We mimicked those scenes when we played cowboy and Indian.

That same year I was in a state of confusion. Mr. Stangl, from the schools Central Office periodically showed up at our school to have us do calisthenics on the playground. Often that included doing squats, so I knew what a squat was. The newspapers and radio news were all about the Police Department using squat cars; at least that's what we thought they were saying.

As we'd walk to and from school, we watched for police cars that would look like some kind of weird squat. It was something of a disappointment when we eventually saw a black sedan looking like any

Art's Odyssey Unplanned

other car, except it had a red light on it, and learned that it was a "squad" car.

Distance was never a factor when I wanted to go somewhere, like Grandma Baker's house on the south side. Busy vehicular traffic, or narrow spaces between streetcars and other traffic, weren't problems as I maneuvered my bike where I wanted to go.

On one excursion to Grandma Baker's place I was riding in the narrow space between parked cars on my right, and an Interurban train on my left just south of Michigan Street on 6th Street. No problem until a guy decides to get out of his car from the driver's seat. My front wheel got him smack in the butt. The Interurban train was moving fast enough so that I was able to quickly bike around the guy without bumping the side of the Interurban, but not fast enough to miss the obscene profanity he yelled.

Another time, seeing the 5:30 p.m. Milwaukee Road west bound commuter train pulling out of the Milwaukee Road Depot just east of the 6th Street Viaduct, I parked my bike at the railing, leaning over it to watch the steam engine come out on the west side of the viaduct. What I got was a face full of the steam from the stack of the locomotive as it picked up speed.

Almost asphyxiated by the impact of the gaseous output, I slid down to the sidewalk, my head spinning. I sat there, getting my breath, for almost an hour before I was able to get up. I walked my bike to the south end of the viaduct before I felt good enough to ride again.

Red's always been my favorite color, and it was appropriate to wear a red sweater to high school, where our colors were red and white. My girlfriend liked red too, and in a weak moment I said she could wear my sweater one day.

She wore it all week, but by the time I got it back, it was obvious that it had taken on the shape of her body, so I wound up giving it to her. Neither of us really minded.

In the second semester of my junior year, I flunked English and chemistry. English because I had real problems with diagramming and didn't do much homework. Chemistry, because I didn't know how to balance chemical equations and again, didn't do the homework. As a result, I had to make it up in summer school at Rufus King High School. I wasn't thrilled at first but as time went on, I enjoyed it.

The English was, it seemed, easier than during the school year; mainly involving reading and reporting on stories that I enjoyed, and chemistry where for the first time we were able to do our own experiments; making us feel like we were real scientists.

It was easier for me to get there and back on my bike than have to pay and wait for streetcars and buses, and I enjoyed the ride. Heading toward home one day, I had to turn from Atkinson Avenue onto 32nd Street.

As I turned, my front wheel got caught in a streetcar track, the bike came to a sudden stop, and I flew over the handle bars to land on my butt on the street, just as a car came whizzing around the curve in the opposite direction. The car missed me, but I had to walk the rest of the way home; the front wheel was too bent to ride. Before the day was over, I had a new front wheel in place.

Art's Odyssey Unplanned

I did learn something besides the periodic tables from chemistry. I got a really sustained anger at the family in general that hot summer and needed some kind of powerfully significant form of revenge. I got it.

Grandpa Schmitz got an idea that he could produce a better fertilizer by making his own. That required digging a huge and deep hole in our back yard; filling it with a combination of fish guts and sulfur, covered with dirt when the hole was full. Then, leaving it sit for some time before digging it up again to find a really good fertilizer.

I loved going along to Smiths Brother's Fish store in Port Washington, even though the part of the business we were looking at smelled strongly of fish guts, etc. They'd fill the containers we brought along with their fish guts that we'd take home to put in Grandpa's fertilizer hole.

That meant we had some leftover sulfur in bags in our basement. I liked to take a little of it, light a match, and watch the blue flame. I also, using something I'd learned in chemistry, slightly cracked a couple of eggs, added a little sulfur, and stashed the eggs on the sand pit on top of our coal fired furnace in the basement.

It didn't take long before my revenge began to take place. The fumes of the hydrogen sulfide coming from the eggs in the basement began to suffuse the house. Everyone was affected, and spent hours of wasted time trying to locate the source of the stinking aroma that didn't subside with all the windows open.

All I had to do was chortle to myself, and spend as much time as possible away from the house, like staying overnight at Bobby's house, without worrying about getting punished or wasting eggs instead of eating them.

Almost from the time Pa got his second car, a '32 Plymouth, we began his annual vacation with a week or two camping, starting at Potawatomi State Park just outside of Sturgeon Bay in Door County. The first time was with a tent Pa'd borrowed from a friend.

By the second year we were hooked on camping at Nicolet Bay at Peninsula State Park just outside of Fish Creek, about 30 miles north of Sturgeon Bay. Bobby always went with us.

Pa'd rent a wooden row boat from a guy in town for $5 a week. Pa'd take us guys out early in the morning for some fishing. The rest of the day I could take the boat out by myself, and in the evening Pa'd take Ma out for some more fishing. Mostly we'd catch nice sized jumbo perch, but there'd be the occasional bass.

We'd often drive down to some cherry orchard near Sturgeon Bay for a day of cherry picking. We'd get a few cents a bucket, but it would add up to give us kids enough to get whatever toy or gimmick we happened to have our eyes on at the time.

One fairly breezy day, I got the folks to let me stay at the campsite instead of going cherry picking. With no particular idea of what I wanted to do, I walked to the beach and sat on the side of the boat, trying to decide whether I wanted to row out to Horseshoe Island again.

Seeing a fairly large and straight branch that was washed up on the beach, I began to explore the possibilities. We had plenty of wash line and

Art's Odyssey Unplanned

there was an old army blanket as well as a number of smaller branches that had been washed up; everything adding up to suggest sailing instead of rowing today.

I rowed about half way out to the island before assembling the branches and blanket to turn the boat into a sailing vessel; an oar serving as a rudder. It worked!

I sang every nautical song I could think of, "Anchors Aweigh," "Sailing, Sailing," etc. My little boat was really moving, and all I had to do was sit there holding the rudder. I was thrilled to pieces. Harold would be ticked off but I was glad he hadn't been with me, and Bobby would have thanked his lucky stars that he wasn't involved; he hated the water.

Eventually, I realized that Nicolet Bay and the island were barely visible in the distance and that it might be a good idea to start heading back while I still could.

I dropped the sail, pulled in the oar, and dropped the hunk of cement that served as an anchor.

My spirits dropped even faster than the anchor when it became clear that the water was deeper than the anchor rope, and the wind was blowing me away from the bay. The only thing I could do was start rowing back to where I started.

Eventually, although painfully slow, I got back to where the anchor began to take hold. By that time I needed a rest. My hands were used to rowing, so I didn't have blisters or anything, but I was tired.

It was a bright sunny day and it was getting hot. After I began to feel better, I knew I needed to cool off, and what better way than to strip and go skinny dipping next to the boat.

Feeling refreshed, I got back in the boat, putting on my pants and shoes, pulled up the anchor and started rowing again. It became painfully obvious that I had to row two yards forward for every one yard I gained; it was going to take me forever to get back, and I had to do that before the gang got back.

I kept at it, but it was getting harder and harder to keep going, but I couldn't quit trying. I was so intent on what I was doing, I hardly noticed the sleek white shape of a 60-foot yacht pulling up next to me.

The next thing I knew was that a long gaff hook was holding my boat against the hull of the yacht. A man on deck started asking me questions about where I'd come from, etc.

A rope ladder was lowered, a line tossed to me with orders to tie it to the bow of my boat, and then I was told to climb the rope ladder to board the yacht. Once on board, I was shown to a dining area and offered a lunch with all the soda I could drink!

With my little boat towed astern of the yacht, we cruised toward Nicolet Bay, where the yachts anchor was dropped. My boat was brought to the side where I climbed down the rope ladder to the boat. The yacht waited till those on board were sure I was going to make it rowing toward shore before weighing anchor.

Beaching the boat, I disposed of the branches I'd used, and put the old blanket where I'd found it. Crawling into the tent I sacked out until the rest of the gang got back from cherry picking. Pa, noticing the boat wasn't in the same spot it had been in, asked where I'd taken the boat. I explained that for the first time I rowed all around Horseshoe Island to the consternation of the seagulls that had their rookery there.

That evening, as usual, Pa drove in to Fish Creek for a few steins of Golden Drops, the local brew. There was a guy at the bar who turned out to be the owner of the yacht that rescued me, and regaled the bar crowd with his version and opinions of my adventure. Pa didn't need a blueprint.

The next morning, Pa took me aside and explained with some painful swats on my butt why I was going to be closely monitored for the remainder of our stay; where the rest of the family went, I was going to be there, plus I was going to be responsible for the after meals clean up, dishes, etc. I think it bothered him that someone might think his son wasn't all there. I got Harold to trade the dishes thing for my cleaning fish he caught.

Once back home, I got together with Ken Isaacson, Ed Kaufman, and a couple of other guys at Ken's place. Ken and his family, living out some rough times, were housed in a tar paper shack a few doors north of our house. Their front door faced another tar paper shack that had been a stable not too many years before. Now it served as a play area for us.

Above the east end was a loft, still with some remnants of hay and a slew of cast off stuff on top of that. This particular day we were having a rubber gun fight; 3 of us on the west side and 3 on the east. There was a variety of stuff we used to hide behind between shots; storage containers, boxes, etc.

With lots of old inner tubes available, all of us had plenty of ammunition for an extended battle. Even if we got hit, it didn't really hurt that much.

We'd been at it awhile when one of my shots went awry and instead of hitting anyone on the east side, it bounced off a big wooden carom board in the loft. The board came down hitting Ed on the head.

A truce was declared immediately. Ed was out cold. He wasn't bleeding or anything, and he was breathing ok, so we just waited for the few minutes it took for him to come to. When he opened his eyes and began to sit up, he started talking.

He wasn't making much sense, but then he usually didn't anyway. It took a few days for the lump on his head to go down.

The day was hot, so we decided on a cease fire while we went out to get some Kool Aid powder, scrounged some ice from Ken's ice box, and fixed up a couple of jars of water with the Kool Aid. After the first jar was gone, the battle began again, but before it did, each side grabbed the rubbers it had shot. That took care of the afternoon until the last jar was empty. Nobody really won, but we had a lot of fun trying.

One hot summer afternoon, Harold, his buddy Bob Gropp, and I took our bikes out to Blatz Park on the Milwaukee River. It was never too hot to race, so once we got to the park, we raced next to each other down the gravel road to the river below.

Going like bats out of blazes at one of the several curves, all of us skidded and fell off our bikes onto the gravel. After a few seconds, we got up and looked at each other to see that we were now a bloody mess of dirty and torn clothes. Figuring we couldn't get much worse, we got back on our bikes and continued our race to the bottom; managing to stay upright on the next curves.

Once at the bottom, we did the only thing we could do to try to make ourselves more presentable at the inevitable return to our homes. Tossing our clothes onto our bikes on the grass we dove naked as jaybirds into the fairly warm water of the slowly moving current of the Milwaukee River.

Then, getting our clothes, we used the river to at least minimize, if not eliminate the bloody stains. There wasn't much we could do about the rips and tears of the fabric, hoping our mothers wouldn't notice too much.

Before we could get dressed, an elderly couple drove down and parked near our bikes. We stayed partly submerged in the water, hoping they wouldn't stay too long.

Whether they caught on to our condition or not, they walked around the area for a few minutes before getting back in their car and headed back up the road. We waited a few minutes before getting out, getting dressed, and getting back on our bikes for the uphill ride to the street and home. With the family pre-occupied with getting set for supper, we got in the house, changed clothes, and enjoyed a good meal with no problems relating to our afternoon.

I was a glutton for less than complimentary nicknames in grade school. I wasn't a fighter. If I complained about problems with other kids, Ma's standard response was "If you're nice to them, they'll be nice to you." Harold on the other hand was more realistic. He was a fighter but he rarely picked a fight.

When I was in 6th grade, Miss Murphy managed to

get Pa to come in for a conference during the week. Her message was that he should make sure we knew how to defend ourselves.

That evening we took the bus and streetcar to Uncle Ollie's house. He was actually Ma's uncle. He and Aunt Clara had two sons quite a bit older than we were and we went home with two sets of regulation boxing gloves.

Harold and I, for the first time were able to fight each other without being scolded. We'd strip to the waist and go at it with the gloves.

Every evening became a boxing event. About a month or so later, Miss Murphy called Pa back for another conference. This time she was quite firm about Pa making sure that we would cease and desist our evening old scores by ganging up on our former abusers.

The problem was that the word didn't get to kids at the 36th Street school where I had to go for manual training. Usually I was able to walk the several blocks north and then back with a friend. But if I was behind in getting my wood work cleaned up before leaving, I was on my own for the return walk.

On one of those occasions, I found myself being chased by several of the 36th street locals. I knew there was no way I could deal with all of them by myself, so I ran.

One thing I could do well was run. Having explored the neighborhood on my own, I knew all the nooks and crannies, free spaces between buildings, and city storage areas between major streets.

As I ran, I experienced a strange satisfaction in the attempt to elude my pursuers. Running east on Villard

Art's Odyssey Unplanned

Avenue, about half way between 36th Street and 35th Street, I ducked between two buildings, purposely slowing down so my pursuers could get closer as we ran. I suddenly realized I had the power to stop the pursuit, and probably future chases as well.

Seemingly out of breath, I was running slower. The first of the guys chasing me suddenly was brought to a painful halt as his stomach connected with the wagon tongue of one of the city's garbage wagons stored in the empty space next to what had been the old fire house. End of chase. It never happened again.

When I was in eighth grade, the folks rented the front bedroom to a woman us kids only knew as Mrs. Shepherd with two daughters; Elaine a freshman in high school, and her younger sister Betty, in 5th grade at Holy Redeemer, the neighborhood catholic school. Because they often ate with us, we got to knew them really well.

Elaine was pretty sharp, but Betty was having all kinds of problems at school. Much of her problem was that nobody at her school with twice as many kids in a class as public school, really tried to help her with things like long division and cursive writing.

I was no whiz at arithmetic, but it didn't take much to show Betty how to deal with remainders in long division. And the cursive writing thing was even easier. She just needed someone to show her how to connect one letter to another when writing anything.

Starting in 6th grade, all the boys had to walk several blocks north to take Manual Training at the 36th Street School. The girls took cooking class at our own school.

I always enjoyed the walk there and back with my friends. It was the class I didn't like. Being much less than well-coordinated, and working only with hand tools, I was at a loss as to how to use a wood plane to square a piece of wood for whatever the project required.

It didn't help that the teacher spent more time telling us about his alleged heroism during the World War than he did trying to help those of us who needed it. The finished projects that I eventually took home were usually completed by my sympathetic friends who understood my problem.

The first shop class in 8th grade was a shocker! As we filed into the room we gasped. Wearing the usual shop apron was an older white haired lady. Her first directive was, "Sit on your work bench."

We couldn't restrain ourselves from verbal speculation about this revolutionary event. Her next command was, "Hold your tongues between your teeth."

Most of us tried to obey her order literally. In a matter of seconds the room was in an uproar of hilarity. That stopped with an audible mass gasp as she wrote her name on the blackboard behind her. Miss Lynch.

After the usual lecture on tool handling safety, Miss Lynch got us started on our first project of the term. She spent almost no time lecturing or talking to the class as a whole, but before the first class of the semester was over, we knew we could count on her for whatever help we needed. For the first time, I was able to complete a fairly involved project, the making of a decorative curio box that would have

Art's Odyssey Unplanned

been totally beyond me in any previous class.

Sixteen! I really didn't think much about it ahead of time, but all of a sudden it dawned on me that, with Pa's help, I could get my driver's license. By the end of October of my sixteenth year, we felt I was ready to take the test for my license.

With Pa at my side I drove, for the first time, downtown to take my test. I thought I was doing pretty good when the cop riding with me told me to stop on the Wells Street hill just east of the City Hall, turn off the engine, use the Emergency Brake, and start the car again without sliding back. I never had the chance to re-start the car.

The cop said, "Drive back to the station, I can't pass you because your Emergency Brake is defective. Come back when that's fixed."

Sometime during the following week, Pa took our '36 Chev Standard 4 door in to have the Emergency Brake repaired. He didn't want to have to take me back downtown after work during the rush hour, so the following Saturday he had me drive to the Shorewood Police Station.

The Shorewood police were openly frank with their opinion that we'd gone there because we thought it'd be easier than Milwaukee. The cop, besides having me do the usual U-turn, Y-turn, and parking routines had me drive to Hubbard Park, down a hill to the shore of the Milwaukee River. That road goes through a narrow double tunnel before coming out near the river's edge.

Once through the first tunnel, the cop had me back up through the tunnel, using only the rear-view mirror. Then, driving back up the hill, stopping the car, turning off the engine, and starting up again with no backward movement, I passed the test.

Seventeen was a great year ranging from desperate frustration to glorious satisfactions during summer vacation.

Robert Gropp, a classmate of Harold's lived a few doors south of us on the other side of the alley. He had no brothers or sisters, so we filled that gap in his life. Besides breeding homing pigeons, he shared our interest in things nautical, with our common tendency to do things without much planning ahead.

It was a mutual decision to build a small wooden scow in Gropp's garage. His Dad was one of the few in the neighborhood who didn't have a car.

We pooled our limited resources to buy the wood, and because of a variety of other demands on our time - I had to go to summer school because I'd flunked English and chemistry - it took us into August before we'd finished our nautical masterpiece, including the caulking and painting a naval grey.

Except for Mud Creek, a shallow stream a few blocks south of us, the nearest water was the Milwaukee River, a couple of miles east of us. We knew better than to ask any of our neighbors or relatives to hook up to a trailer to haul our boat to the river.

On launch day, we gingerly managed to get our boat up on our coaster wagon and began the careful, slow walk to the river. It took us the better part of the day to get to a creek that ran into the river. Easing our boat off the wagon into the creek, we had to use the oars to push the boat over the shallow water until we finally reached the river, leaving the wagon at the launch site.

Art's Odyssey Unplanned

Taking turns rowing around the area, it dawned on us that we had to find a place to stow the boat until we could establish a permanent mooring place for it. The Milwaukee County Park Commission had just put up a Casting Pier on the east bank of the river.

Rowing to it, we found that with the three of us sitting on the pier and pushing our feet on the bow, we could ease the boat under the pier, and with it squeezed tightly between the water and the pier it wasn't going anywhere. Our coaster wagon was still where we'd left it, as we walked back home.

Later that day we got Pa to drive us over to the casting pier to show him our boat.

He was almost as stunned as we were to find no sign of it under the pier.

Lowering ourselves into the water while hanging onto the pier, we tried to see if there was any sign of our boat anywhere under the pier. We finally left the place, now convinced that someone took advantage of the situation to get themselves a ready-made boat.

The next day, the three of us explored the area on the east side of the river trying to see if we could find any sign of our boat. No luck at all.

The second day Pa took the bus to work, and left the keys to our '36 Chev so I could spend the day checking out the west bank of the river; that side being full of privately owned waterfront properties. With Harold and Gropp along to look while I drove, we slowly perused the shoreline of the west bank. It was late in the afternoon when we found evidence indicating the location of our boats thieves. Unfortunately, it was large pieces of grey painted wood that told us the story.

Hurrying home, I got on the phone to call the Milwaukee County Sheriff's office. Explaining the situation, we agreed to meet a deputy at the scene. The upshot was that the father of the young boys who'd destroyed our work agreed, as if he had a choice, to meet us in the Sheriff's office the next day with his sons.

Taking the bus and streetcar, Gropp, Harold, and I went to Sheriff Schinners office where the culprits were already seated in front of the Sheriff's desk. The sheriff had us explain our side of the story, including the work, the hours, and the successful result being our boat.

Then, explaining to the father and his three sons, the implications of what they had done in terms of possible penalties, he read them the riot act about their chances of severe punishment. Sheriff Schinners went on to explain that a large fine could be invoked with a sentence of the boys to the Detention Home. His voice shaking, the father explained that they were living in the shack on the river because he was out of work. By this time, the kids were crying and their father's hands were shaking.

The Sheriff ordered them to sit out in an antechamber while he spoke to us. "Boys, you guys weren't too smart to leave your boat where you did, but I have to make sure those people understand that they can't just go out and destroy property that belongs to someone else. In order to do that, I have to ask you how much money you spent on the materials for the boat."

We hadn't kept any records of the cost of the wood, caulking, nails, and paint, but we were finally

Art's Odyssey Unplanned

able to determine that we'd spent $10.00 plus all the hours we spent putting it all together, and that's what we told the Sheriff.

"Boys," the Sheriff said, "I'm going to call those fellows back in here and assign a penalty for what they did. You have to realize, I can't charge them for the time and labor you put into the boat, and because there was no specific identification that showed the boat belonged to you, I'm limited in what I can do about it."

"If you don't like my decision, you can ask that this case go to Juvenile Court where the odds are great that because these kids have no previous record, they'll be put on a short period of probation and you'll get nothing. So, here's what I'm going to do, and I'd advise all three of you to accept it when I ask if this is okay with you."

"I'm going to say that if the father can pay you $10 cash right now, the boys will be released to the custody of the father, and they'll be free to go home, where I suspect the father will add to the penalty."

The little group was called in. The Sheriff repeated the seriousness of the charges, the possibility of a Juvenile Court appearance and a sentence to the Detention Home if the penalty he was going to impose couldn't be met.

"Sir," he said, "I have discussed the situation with the three young men whose boat your boys stole and wrecked. They've put a lot of hard work and time building that boat, and spent their own money on the materials. If, Sir, you can immediately pay these young men the $10 they spent, I will consider this case closed."

Rising from his chair, the father took out his wallet and taking out a fiver and five ones handed it in our direction. Harold took it, forcing himself to say "Thank you." The other boys had sheer panic on their faces as they left the room. We weren't overjoyed, but figured we'd at least got something out of it, even if it was only $3.33+ for each of us.

Camping at Peninsula State Park, we'd come to know the Redman family from Chicago. We had a standing invitation to visit them.

That year, 1939, Ma and Pa rented a bedroom to Leo and Jack Gehl. Leo was running a floral delivery service from our house, but the rest of his family lived in Chicago. Weekends, Leo and Jack took turns going to be with the family in Chicago.

One fall weekend, Jack took Harold and I along on his drive home. Leaving right after school we were in Chicago in time for supper. Right after we'd eaten, Jack left to go out with his girlfriend.

I asked Jack's mother if it would be okay for me to walk down Kenneth St. and take the Irving Park streetcar west, over to the Redman's house. With her okay, I was on my way. Harold stayed with the Gehl's.

The Redman parents were home, but the rest of the family had all gone out. I was disappointed, but it was still too early to go back to the Gehl's house. I hopped an east bound Irving Park streetcar, riding it to where it connected with the Sheridan Road L train, and took that to the loop.

It was a beautiful fall evening, cool enough to be crisp between the skyscrapers rising above the sparkling sidewalks leading me to wherever. I knew

Art's Odyssey Unplanned

there was a railroad with stops near the Gehl's house, and learned that I could actually take a train from the Northwestern Depot, getting off at the Ravenswood stop, and walk the short distance to the Gehl house on Kenneth.

Thrilled to the bone with my first foray alone in Chicago, I'd lost all track of time, and hadn't realized the concern the Gehl family felt about my safety being alone in Chicago, but being duly contrite, I was first forgiven, and then congratulated on being able to cope as I did without a guide.

We'd had a program in the auditorium. It was a dull lecture about who knows what, so I slumped in my seat and day dreamed about more exciting details of life while the speaker droned on and on and on.

During my first class after lunch, I was summoned to the office of our School Advisor whose job was, besides arranging schedules, to put the fear of God into any kind of student misbehavior. "Arthur," he intoned as he glared at me, "I have a note from Mrs. Royal concerning your rowdy conduct during the program this morning. As a penalty, I'm sending you to the library where you'll write a 2,000-word theme to be handed in to Mrs. Royal before you leave school today. Now, get going."

I left his office in a high dudgeon of righteous indignation! He hadn't given me a subject, leaving me free to compose a theme that would express my feelings about this gross miscarriage of scholastic justice. Particularly aimed at Mrs. Royal, my dissertation on fossils covered all educators as well.

It was almost 4 p.m. when I presented my work to the man who'd assigned it. Without a glance at it, he told me, "Take it to Mrs. Royal, she's the one who reported you."

As I walked into the room, Mrs. Royal asked, "Arthur, what are you doing in the building this late?" Tossing my work on her desk, I said, "This is what Mr. M. told me to do because you reported me for misbehaving during the assembly this morning."

As she began to read my writing about fossils, she almost screamed, "Come with me," and picking up the paper, she tore out of the room, explaining that I wasn't the one she'd reported, she'd reported Andrew Schmidt. Reaching Mr. Mark's office, she said, "Wait here," as she barged into his office.

I couldn't resist chortling in glee to myself as Mrs. Royal, shredding every layer of dignity, tore into Mr. Marks. All of a sudden, my work of the afternoon was worth everything I'd put into it.

Her tirade went on and on, and I didn't hear a sound out of Mr. High and Mighty. Finally, as quiet took place, Mrs. Royal came out and putting her arm on my shoulder, told me how sorry she was that I'd been wrongly involved, and that to clear things up, I'd be excused from any homework in her class for the next 30 days, but that she had to add, how well written my theme had been.

As a freshman, I took Mr. Parker's citizenship class. As Mr. Parker lectured at the front of the room, I felt a sting on my cheek as a paper wad, shot from across the room by one of my buddies, hit me. With neither of us particularly interested in the lecture, I felt justified in evening the score.

Carefully folding a small piece of paper, then bending it in the middle, and carefully placing it in

Art's Odyssey Unplanned

the center of a rubber band stretched between two fingers of my left hand, I pulled it back for maximum tension before letting it go.

It flew straight toward my target on the other side of the room, but half way there, my paper wad made a sharp right turn, striking Mr. Parker in the cheek as he'd begun to walk down the aisle between the two last rows of desks. Still, with the now limp rubber band between my fingers, I was sent to the office with a note asking the principal to suspend me.

It was still mid-morning on a beautiful fall day, so I figured I could endure the reaction from the folks in return for a 3-day break from school. Walking in the front door, Ma asked, "What're you doing home at this time of the day?" Handing her the suspension note, I went into the kitchen for a snack.

A few minutes later, she sat down next to me at the table and handed me the suspension note with an order to read what she'd written on the other side.

"Dear sir, I send my son to school to get the education my taxes are paying for. Please admit him to his classes, and I will be happy to meet with you at 3:15 this afternoon. Thank you,

Mrs. A. Schmitz."

"Now, get going. You can finish your snack when you get home this afternoon." I stopped at Shorty's restaurant on Villard Avenue for a burger, and then at Wilbert's bakery on the corner of 37th and Villard for dessert before getting back to school.

At 3:15, Ma and I entered the principal's office. We'd barely got the formal courtesy preliminaries out of the way, when another kid came in and said they needed me on the stage of the Auditorium. I was a member of the stage crew of our drama club. To my surprise, the principal excused me. I have no idea what Ma and Mr. W. talked about, but that was the last I heard about my problem of the morning in citizenship class.

It was customary for any public performance by the band, orchestra, chorus, or drama club to charge an admission of 25 or 50 cents a ticket. Our family was always good about not only buying the tickets for everyone, but actually going to the performance. Usually, whoever was living with us at the time also bought tickets and attended the event.

For one of the plays I was involved with, the seats for the family and Ray and Catherine Thomas were split between rows P and Q in the auditorium. At supper the night before, we were discussing who'd sit where. Sis surprised the rest of us when she firmly declared, "I wanna sit in P with the Thomas's."

Mrs. Royal's homeroom had a unique feature. Knowing how much we all loved using colored chalk instead of the usual white, we were told that each week a different pupil could draw anything that was desired with colored chalk on the blackboard at the back of the room. The one exception was that we weren't allowed to draw the flag of any country.

One of my curiosities was seeing what the flags of other countries looked like. I spent hours with the encyclopedias in the library. I knew what the flags of England, France, Germany, and Canada looked like, but there were so many others that I'd never seen.

I had mixed feelings about doing it, but one week I had to tell Mrs. Royal that the current design on the blackboard was the flag of Liberia. When asked how

Art's Odyssey Unplanned

I knew that, I got permission from the librarian to bring the F encyclopedia down to the homeroom. Mrs. Royal complimented the artist on his imagination, but his design had to be erased.

A couple of weeks later, it was my turn to do the design. Using every color there was, I created a montage of squares, circles, and triangles, with some inner circles and squares filled in with contrasting colors.

One wintry day before Harold and Sis got promoted to high school, I noticed a thermometer on the wall outside of Wilbert's Bakery. I knew in a vaguer sort of way that water froze at 32 degrees above zero, and how it felt when the mercury shot up into the 90's. Now for the first time I saw the real temperature that was below freezing at 28 degrees. Every day after that I checked the temperature to see exactly how cold or hot it was at that particular time.

Most kids have been warned about talking to strangers, and I was no exception, but hey, there are strangers and there are strangers. When I was around 10 or 11, me and my buddy Paul Van Luven walked over to the Milwaukee Road depot just off Cameron Avenue.

There was a small switch engine on a side track where the old white haired engineer had stopped for a smoke break. He gave us a cheerful "goot mornink, boyss" with a strong, I guessed German accent, so I replied, "Wie gehts, mein herr."

He lit up like a Christmas tree! "Vould you boyss like a rite in mine engine?" he asked! He'd barely got the words out of his mouth before we finished climbing the steps to the cab of the engine.

Following us up, he sat on the left side of the cab with us seated on the right, he backed the engine off the spur and on to the main line.

Once on the main line, he ran us forward up the track. It wasn't a smooth ride, but we couldn't have cared less as we passed the local crossings we knew, 37th St., Villard Ave., past Silver Spring and out into the countryside as we steamed our way northwest up the track.

After about 5 miles, our engineer slowed the engine to a brief stop before putting it in reverse and backing down the track to the little depot where we got off with profuse, "Viel danke's."

Paul and I separated there, to run home without our feet touching the ground to share our thrilled pleasure with the first person we'd see at home. Both of us were knocked to the ground by our mothers as we told them of our adventure. In my case, Ma was strident in her case about not only talking to strangers, but accepting rides with them- especially railroad men! That hurt. At least for the next ten minutes or so.

Not long after that, Kenny Isaacson, Harold and I went for a hike on a nice Saturday. We walked to the Milwaukee River where we stopped for an impromptu picnic of sorts. We'd come prepared.

Using only our hands, we dug a hole in the soft soil at the bank, scrounged up some small and fairly dry branches to put in the hole. We lit them, wrapped the couple of potatoes we'd brought in silver paper, and put them on top of the burning wood. We left them there for a while, before taking them out, peeling off the silver paper, and eating them. They tasted pretty good, and we washed them down by cupping our hands in the river and drinking what we could that way.

We felt like real pioneers. Even though the river was right there, it was more fun to put our fire out by playing what we called "church on fire." We solved two problems at the same time. We didn't need a bathroom till we got home, and we got the fire out.

Part 2

After graduating from probably the only high school named after a loser, I hit the Help Wanted lists in the daily paper. One of the jobs I got was being a helper on a Goodwill truck. Weighing about 90 pounds, it was hard going helping some big lug of a guy haul an overstuffed sofa down three flights of steps then loading it into the truck.

After doing that for a few weeks, the boss told me I was being re-assigned to work in the shop with the same pay. Working with the others in the shop, our job was to convert burlap bags into useable packing material, nothing to it.

It was obvious that my co-workers had a variety of problems; physical and mental, but they were the most cheerful and friendly people I'd ever met. It was a real pleasure working with them.

After two weeks, the boss called me into his office. "Arthur," he said. "We took you off the truck because it was clear you couldn't handle the heavy stuff. Then we assigned you to this job, rather than firing you, because we hoped you'd quit, but you didn't, so I have to tell you we're letting you go. You can pick up your check at the pay window, and good luck."

It didn't take too long to find another job. This one was really different – to me at least. It was a 2nd shift

Art's Odyssey Unplanned

job at an insulation factory below the Forest Home Ave. bridge. My job was to load the finished product, bundles of insulation destined for Army barracks, onto box cars at the siding. The pay was good, the bundles weren't all that heavy, and it was something I could do. And then came the, but?

I'd get home during the wee hours, buses and streetcars only ran every hour during the night. I'd have to take a bath and change, because my clothes and hair were permeated with loose red fibers from the insulation bundles. I quit when after a few weeks I was coughing up the stuff.

My 5th grade teacher, for whatever reason, asked me to write a poem to go with a kitchen tool she was giving as a gift to a friend who was getting married. I started out with the old saying, "The way to a man's heart is through his stomach" and went on from there. She told me it wasn't quite what she had in mind, but told me later she'd used it anyway and it was the hit of the gift opening thing.

For some reason or other, my 6th grade teacher, Mrs. Timble, kept me after school one afternoon. With nothing to do, I sat at my desk eyeballing the railroad tracks just east of the building. I didn't think about me being the only one kept after school that day. After about ten minutes, Mrs. Timble said, "Arthur, you haven't been your usual active self today. I think I'll let you go home now, and maybe you'll feel better tomorrow." Boy, did I feel better as soon as I got out the last door!

For Washington's birthday, Mrs. Timble had us learn to dance the Virginia Reel and come to school that day wearing costumes like they wore in those days; the girls wearing long skirts and caps and us guys dressed in black suits of the time, some of us sporting wigs as well. I loved the dancing part.

I was never sure what brought the comment on, but one day Mrs. Timble told me, "Arthur, wild elephants couldn't make you do something you didn't want to do, but you can be led by a silk string." I guess.

Partly because they were cheaper, but partly because I liked the idea of knowing a foreign stamp had actually been used, I preferred to buy or trade for stamps that were canceled. My friend Tommy Brisgal became a great source of canceled stamps from faraway places.

I never questioned his sources; I was just happy to be able to get canceled stamps from other parts of the world. It was by accident that one day I noticed a similarity between stamps I'd just bought from Tommy. One was from the British Leeward Islands, and the other was from New Caledonia; two places thousands of miles apart and from two different colonial powers. Both stamps had the same identical cancellation!

Suddenly the light dawned. Tommy's father was a cigar maker, and each box when filled required a U.S. Revenue stamp to be affixed and canceled. My recent prizes it turned out, had the U.S. cancellation. Rather than admit that I'd been had, I simply stopped buying or trading with Tommy, still enjoying his company as a friend.

It was in 7th grade that our school got the word that we were to put on a gymnastics field day that would be attended by the big wigs from the Central

Office. Usually I liked the kind of things we'd be doing; mostly calisthenics involving our arms and legs.

But, being kept after school to develop the kind of perfection Ol lady Murphey wanted was a real turn-off for me. That was MY time!

She'd seen me in action on the playground, so she didn't like it that my distance doing the broad jump was less, a lot less than I could do. It became a contest of wills.

Each jump I did at her command turned out to be less than the one before. She was a lot more concerned about the standings of the school than I was. The big difference between us was that I was enjoying the situation. I was the only one who could decide how far I would jump. I had the distinct feeling that she was too close for her comfort to keep from giving me a swat on the butt, which made it all the more delightful for me. And, as time and repetitions went by, I began to realize she wanted to end the day here even more than I did.

Finally, the old lady got up from the chair she'd been using and called me over. "Arthur, I will see you in my office at morning recess tomorrow. You can take this chair inside." She looked daggers at me when she saw that I got a kid in 6th grade to take her chair inside.

The next day she had to send another kid out on the playground to remind me that I was supposed to be in her office during recess. I waited till the bell rang before I went to her office, meaning I was able to avoid doing any class work while I was there.

7th grade turned to be great. We had Miss Lassen for our teacher. At 12 we could appreciate feminine beauty, and Miss Lassen qualified. Eddy Chesnick and I both loved to sing. Eddy's goal in life was to be a popular professional vocalist with his own radio show and concert performances. My goal was to be a lecturer like those I enjoyed at the museum.

Eddy managed to get Miss Lassen ticked off, so I was the one chosen to sing in the biennial Music Festival at the Milwaukee Auditorium. I was more than thrilled to be among 2,000 other participants and thoroughly enjoyed the fringe benefits. One was getting out of school to go to rehearsals during a school day. Some of the rehearsals took place at Washington High School. To get there, I had to take the Green Bus. This was a first for anyone in our family. The Green Bus was operated by the Wisconsin Motor Coach Company, and required extra fare; not accepting the paper transfers or passes of the TMR&L system operating the rest of the buses and streetcars in the city.

The evening of our performance, we assembled in the basement of the auditorium until it was time to go on stage. That's when I met the first black kid to talk to. Everett was a 7th grader at Vieau School, and we really hit it off. Our concert, of course, was a huge success that had me on cloud nine for days afterward.

By 1940, the depression was abating; however, being very much a minor, I only knew that money was in very scarce supply, especially for frivolous expenditures such as hobby items. Ma and Pa had always been supportive of my penny-ante stamp collecting purchases because after all, this was educational.

That year the post office issued a new set of what

Art's Odyssey Unplanned

collectors called definitives, the ordinary postage stamps, as compared to those commemorating something special. The highest value of the new set was the $5 President Coolidge stamp. I'd managed to get the $1 and $2 stamps without anyone else knowing, but $5 for a single stamp!

I spent sleepless nights, while Harold snored as he slept, trying to find a way to get that stamp mint - that is unused. Getting that stamp became an obsession. I needed that stamp to complete the set.

My income of 50 cents a week plus my allowance of 25 cents figured out to an interminable wait of more than a couple of months. Beating the bushes among the neighbors for paying chores, I managed to more than double my income.

After some time, with $5 in my pocket, I took the bus and streetcar to the Philatelic Window at the main post office downtown on East Wisconsin Ave. The clerk took my money and slid my prize across the marble counter into my eager hands.

I reveled in a glow of satisfaction as I kept looking at what was already the most valuable stamp in my collection. Ma was home when I walked through the front door.

"You look awfully pleased with yourself," was her opening comment. Ma had often expressed her sympathy and admiration for the way Calvin Coolidge had dealt with the death of his son, so I thought I could safely share my good news.

"Ma," I said, "I bought a picture of Calvin Coolidge," and headed for our room.

"Wait a minute, I want to see that picture." I took the stamp out of the glassine envelope and put it on the dining room table. Ma bent over to look at my "picture." I kept going to our room.

"Hey, wait a minute Buster, that's a stamp!" I agreed. Almost screaming, she yelled, "That's a FIVE-dollar stamp!" Without stopping for breath, she went on, "Where'd you get that stamp, and take it back right now, and get your money back!"

Almost in tears, I did a rare thing in our house. I yelled back. "Ma, I got it at the main post office, they don't take stamps back, and they're closed, and besides I need it to complete the set," which I knew was Greek to Ma.

Of course, I had to explain in detail, how and where I got the money and how could I be so foolish as to spend that much on a piece of paper, when I knew of all the other really important things I really needed, and on and on. Pa was more understanding and eventually the storm blew over.

The summer of 1941 was energetic to say the least. Harold, his friend Robert Gropp, and I heard about a job gathering Sugar Beets at a farm just north of Silver Spring Road, easy to get to on our bikes. We were hired even though we thought the pay was too low for the work it took pulling the beets out of the ground, shucking the leaves off, and putting the beets in bushel baskets.

We worked in small groups. Sometimes, to fill a basket faster, we'd fill it with leaves with a layer of two of beets on top. Another nearby group began taunting us with profane slurs, so we retaliated by throwing a few beets at them.

They did the same, and before long we had a real beet battle going on. That's when the supervisor

Art's Odyssey Unplanned

came out and fired the other group. By that time, we'd had it, and we quit.

Robert's Dad moonlighted by umpiring semi-professional baseball games, so it wasn't long before the three of us got jobs delivering baseball score cards.

We'd bike it to an empty lot near 16th and Center mid-afternoon, and wait for the boss to arrive with the score cards containing all the up-to-the minute details of both major leagues.

While waiting for the score cards, we'd have trick bike riding contests. It was sheer luck that nobody got hurt. We had special baskets for our bikes to hold the 14 by 18 inch cards while we delivered them from one tavern to another en route to our homes. The job was easier than the beet farm, more fun, and paid a lot better - with fringe benefits of a free soda or two at some of the taverns.

My cousin Dorothy got married in August of '41. The party was held at our house and was still going strong at 3 a.m. the next day. Harold and I'd been partying till then, but left to join Kenny Isaacson. By 3:30 a.m., Kenny, Harold, and I were on our bikes heading northwest on Fond Du Lac Avenue which was also Highway 55. Bobby was supposed to go with us but chickened out. A few miles out of town we came to Meeker's Hill. It was so steep, some of the older model cars had to use reverse to ascend it so there'd be no interruption of gas flow to the engine from the tank.

That hill was our first challenge, and it became a point of honor that we'd not walk our bikes up any hill we came to.

The night was warm and it began to rain. We were

free to do whatever we wanted, so who cared. We had some sodas in a kind of saddle bag hung over the rear wheel. When we stopped to rest and wet our whistle, we emptied the saddle bags on the grass next to the road. All the glass bottles were broken

We rode out on 55 and turned west on 60 to start the west leg of our trip. At each town we'd stop at whatever greasy spoon was open and have a burger and a cup of coffee. It had finally stopped raining.

Traffic had been light but began picking up after the sun rose and dried us up. We'd been pretty well soaked. Our longest stop was at Lodi where we had a couple of hamburgers and coffee, before heading out on a county highway to a place on Lake Wisconsin, a wide part of the Wisconsin River. We were headed for an empty lot Ken's uncle owned.

It was 10 p.m. that evening when we got there. Ken's Dad, with Bobby along, had hauled, and pitched the tent we'd be using, and had a nice fire going with a hot meal ready for us.

All we had to do when we got there was eat again, and soon after, wave good byes to the guys as they drove off. There were a lot of bushes around, and leaves on the ground, so we had no problems when we had to go either way.

We always had a campfire, but we always put it out before we sacked out for the night. Although close to the water, it was more fun to put the fire out without going to the river for water. Harold and Kenny broke up when I said, "How about that, we were born with our own fire extinguishers."

Our first night there, we slept with nothing on. After that we slept in our underwear and pants.

Art's Odyssey Unplanned

There were places we didn't want mosquito bites.

We had few if any problems, and those we did have were less than significant. We caught some nice fish one evening and put them in an old burlap bag we put in the lake till the next day, but by morning, turtles had bitten through the bag and eaten our catch.

After that, we'd clean and cook our fish right after we caught them, and we did that often. We caught some nice bass, crappies, bluegills, and perch. The bass gave us the best fight. We'd use some of the fish guts for bait.

With our bikes, we explored the area, from atop the cliffs overlooking Devil's Lake to riding the free ferry from our side of Lake Wisconsin to Merrimac on the other side. We didn't encounter any of the reputedly most poisonous rattle snakes known to be in the area of the cliffs.

We rode over to Devils Lake State Park and swam at the beach there. When we knew our neighbors weren't around, we'd dispense with trunks when we swam at the lot.

Periodically we'd hear strange booming noises from some distant location, which we were told was Artillery at Camp McCoy. Later we learned the booming sounds were from sand blasting a few miles away.

In the evening we'd visit the folks in the cabin on the lot adjoining ours. Their daughter Lorraine, the same age I was, also had a stamp collection. I started dating her after we got home.

We'd heard there were free movies on the square in Merrimac on Tuesday evenings. It rained most of that day, so the wood for our fire was pretty damp and hard to start. But with a kerosene lamp it wasn't a problem to squirt some on the fire we needed to heat up the pork and beans we were having for supper.

As we ate, I told the guys my serving tasted like kerosene. Theirs didn't. By the time we were ready to head for the ferry, I had the damnedest belly ache, but I wasn't going to miss the movie, or stay at our camp alone, so I biked in with the others.

We got there in time for the show, sat on the grass, and my gut was killing me, but I watched the movie. About half way through the flick, all of a sudden I felt great! Instantly I was able to enjoy the movie. About the same time, we noticed everyone was moving as far away from me as they could get, while Harold and Ken were laughing it up.

A week later, we hated to leave the free and easy life we'd been enjoying, but our food supply had dwindled down to next to nothing, and we didn't have a lot of spare cash left for the homeward trip. We had it a little better going back.

We left after daylight in the morning, knowing Kenny's Dad and Bobby'd be coming out to clear our campsite. Heading east from Lodi, we had a couple of interesting episodes.

A small dog was racing us on the north side of the highway. With its eyes on us, it didn't see a close to the ground metal advertising sign, running smack into it with a loud metallic echo. We stopped riding for a minute or two because we were laughing so hard. Not too much further, a couple of police dogs, as we called them, came after us. We were prepared for attacks like that. We each had squirt guns filled

Art's Odyssey Unplanned

with Ammonia instead of water. That took care of the situation very nicely.

We noticed that our homeward trek was quite a bit easier because more of it was downhill. With Kenny wanting to get home in time for the first showing of a movie that evening at the Ritz, we didn't stop much for refreshments on our way home.

It was still light when we rode onto 38th Street, but we were all too tired to take in a movie that evening.

I always had a hard time doing homework. I mean, why should I spend hours copying stuff from books when I was getting A's on tests and exams because I knew the stuff? Anyway, the result was spending time at Mr. M's office instead of being in class.

There were two such occasions that triggered some interesting reactions from Mr. M, the so-called school advisor. One was, when in his deepest bass tone he asked, "Schmitz, should I pray for you?" Although seething inside, I calmly replied, "I have no objection." For some reason, he lost it! He slammed his fist so hard, he actually cracked the glass covering the top of his desk before he yelled "Go back to your class."

There was another time when a lot of my friends in the same boat were standing on the few steps outside his office. Mr. M. made the error of telling me, "Schmitz, you're standing on your last leg." That triggered a group laugh from the bunch outside who understood a totally different meaning than Mr. M. intended.

Again, his temper got the best of him. He got up from behind his desk, slammed the open door so hard, it cracked the glass window on the upper part of the door.

Toward the end of my Junior year, I was summoned to Mr. Marck's office to hear him tell me I was going to have to take Biology 2 over again, adding "You'd have to write a 95 grade on the final exam to pass that course." I wrote a 97 on the final.

Toward the end of my Senior year, Mr. Friedenberg, my Physics teacher asked me to see him after school one day. "Schmitz" he said, "I'm going to have to flunk you. Anyone whose had even one semester of Algebra should be able to figure out the material we've been doing." I told him, "Mr. Friedenberg, I've never had Algebra."

"How come Mr. Marks even let you take Physics." "I don't know, but I've enjoyed the class and the material even if I couldn't figure out the math stuff."

"Schmitz, even without that, you've been performing way over your head. I can't flunk you, but I can't give you more than a D grade, but that'll let you graduate with your class. Good luck."

I'd heard Pa and his friends talk about a place called Rugby Junction. I was between jobs after graduation and learned that a train stopping at the Milwaukee Road's North Milwaukee station went there. So, one bright, warm, sunny, summer morning I walked over to the depot to buy a ticket to Rugby Junction.

The ticket agent said, "You don't wanna go there, there's nothing there!" Insisting that I did wanna go there, he sold me the round-trip ticket I asked for."

A few minutes later I climbed aboard the little two passenger car train with a choice of a lot of empty seats.

The conductor, with a funny look at me, punched

Art's Odyssey Unplanned

my ticket. Except for the ride in a switch engine when I was a kid, I'd never ridden north on a train before. Once in the country, everything looked bright and shiny after the heavy rain of the night before.

All too soon, it was only an hour after I boarded, the train slowed to let me step off. This was Rugby Junction. Now I knew why it was called Rugby Junction; at least as far as the 'Junction' part was concerned.

The Ticket Agent at the station was almost completely right. Standing next to the track I saw my train disappearing in the distance. This was a place where the tracks of the Milwaukee Road and the Chicago and Northwestern Road crossed, hence the Junction label.

Except for a kind of watch tower between the two sets of tracks, the ticket agent was right. There was nothing there. Knowing there wouldn't be a train going back to Milwaukee till early evening, I had to figure out what to do next.

I climbed a perfectly vertical ladder to the tower to see if there was any kind of road I could reach for a ride back to town. From the top I saw a fairly busy road a fair distance to the east.

Once back down, I started my hike eastward. I hadn't planned on any kind of trek through a wilderness of tall wet grasses and wild shrubs, so it was slow going. With time passing it began to get hot. I'd figured on getting something at a restaurant when I got to Rugby Junction, so I didn't have anything to eat or drink with me.

The ground wasn't level, so I'd be climbing small mounds of earth before sliding down the other side.

On one of those, I slipped on the wet ground, winding up sitting in a good size puddle. I had to get down on all fours to maneuver my way up again.

Crawling up on the next mound, I stood still trying to decide what I should do next, although I really didn't have much choice. With no one around, I wasn't worried about taking all my clothes off, to wring them out as much as possible, but hadn't thought of providing various forms of flying insect life including mosquitos with a free lunch counter.

The shocker was the pollywogs flopping back into the water when I took my under shorts off. I made a stab at wringing my clothes out before deciding it'd be better to let them dry on me while moving toward the road I'd seen.

Without a watch I had no idea of how much time was passing, but there was no way I could move as fast as I wanted to. Eventually I did get to the road that turned out to be U.S. Highway 41.

Knowing I must have looked like the lowest dregs of society, I saw no other way of getting home any time soon without waving my thumb in the air, while continuing to walk on the shoulder of the south bound lane of the highway, hoping and praying some kind soul would take a chance on me.

Finally! It happened. An old geezer driving a beat up old 1930 Nash sedan pulled over and waved me in to his jalopy. As we pulled away, I started to silently pray again. Sure, I was getting a ride, but this guy was stewed to the gills, weaving all over the road as we rode toward town.

We got to Silver Spring Road, and I asked him

Art's Odyssey Unplanned

if he could turn east and drop me off at Hopkins Street. I'm not sure if he was honest, but he said, "Yeah, I'm goin' that way anyway." It was going on 4 o'clock when I got on a 59 bus at the end of the line.

There were a lot of people on the bus, but I found a seat. Folks sitting in front of me and behind me decided to move to other places on the bus. I couldn't help but laugh to myself at what I thought of as a Lifeboy moment. That was a soap advertised on the radio as the cure for BO; body odor.

Getting home, I managed to sneak in the back door, get to my bedroom, pick up some clean clothes, and take a bath before anyone else in the family saw me.

What I couldn't hide at the supper table was my sunburned face and arms. I explained that by telling everyone I'd gone for a hike up the train tracks that crossed Hopkins street and walked to the bridge one could see a few miles up the line.

One of the popular songs during my junior year in high school was "Ya Gotta be a Football Hero, to Get a Beautiful Gal." Neither me or any of my friends played on the team, but that didn't stop us from trying to at least be able to handle a football.

One afternoon, Harold, our friend Bob Gropp, and I were tossing a football around in our living room. We were doing pretty well until I passed it to Bob and Harold tried to intercept and the football connected with the globe around Ma's favorite floor lamp, smashing it to pieces.

None of us had much money, and we didn't know how much time we had, but making sure we cleaned up every last smidgeon of the mess, we pooled our resources, hopped on our bikes and headed to Storck's Hardware Store. There, miracle of miracles we were able to buy an exact duplicate of the globe for sixty-eight cents, head back to the house, and put it in, just minutes before Ma got home from work. In the meantime, Bob had put the football in the basket of his bike.

By the time I was a Senior in high school, I'd outgrown my swimming suit, so Bob and I went shopping for new trunks. At the time, Harold and I were sharing a pull-out day bed in the dining room, and Sis had the rear bedroom, but that was where Bob and I got into our new trunks before modeling them for the family in the parlor.

There happened to be a small bottle of Sis's Lilly of the Valley on the chifforette in the bedroom. On a spur of the moment kind of thing, Bob baptized me with a goodly share of Lilly of the Valley. As we paraded ourselves in front of the family, Sis suddenly lost her temper at the whiff she got of her perfume. Beating a fast trip to the bathroom, we locked ourselves in until we were assured by others that they'd toss our clothes in to us.

"Beans, beans, the musical fruit, the more you eat, the more you toot!" or so the song began. Sis loved Ma's pork and beans. Harold and I didn't, until one evening we realized Ma was almost out of them.

At supper that evening, both of us asked Ma for more for ourselves. Ma, ever pleased when we'd ask for more of anything we ate, was more than happy to oblige and we got the last batch available that evening, so nobody got seconds. Sis knew why we did it, and told Ma as much. Ma didn't say a word in

Art's Odyssey Unplanned

reply. The strange thing was that after that Harold and I realized we also liked Ma's Pork and Beans.

I was 12 years old when my pal Kenny wanted me to go downtown with him one Saturday afternoon. The day before I'd made a mess in the basement, and Pa was more than a little put out about it.

"You can go," Pa said, "But not before you clean all the basement windows on the outside." More than a little mad about the delay, I tried to speed up the process by splashing each window with water tossed from a small can. It actually worked pretty well on the windows on one side of the house.

I got distracted by hearing the sirens of the fire engines on Hopkins Street, so that on the second window of the back of the house, the can slipped out of my hand as I tossed the water toward the window, with the can smashing right through the window, nearly hitting Pa in the head in the basement.

A minute later, Pa came out the back door with the can in his hand. "You won't be going anywhere until that window is replaced," he snarled. "Forget the rest of the windows until after you've fixed the one you broke. Now get going!"

A few minutes later, Kenny came over, saying, "I gotta go now, I can't wait no more." I was too mad at myself to cry, and completely stymied as to how to do something I had no idea about where to start.

I didn't care much for the man next door, but he was a carpenter and maybe he could tell me what I needed to know. He turned out to be really nice about it. He lent me a tape measure, and jotted down a step-by-step set of directions as he told me what to ask for at the hardware store.

Armed with his simple manual, I walked the six blocks to Storcks Hardware store to get the glass and window putty I needed. I didn't know how much it would cost, but Mr. Storck said I could pay a quarter a week until it was paid up. That was my total allowance a week!

The tough part was getting the rest of the old glass out to make room for the new window. After that, things went pretty well, but by the time I was finished, I wasn't going anywhere except supper and then to bed. I was pooped.

It was in my Junior year when I was summoned to the office of Mr. Marks. Now what, was my thought as I mounted the several steps to his office. "Schmitz" he began, "some of us are concerned about what seems to be an element missing from your social life, and a need to teach you some greater sense of responsibility, so we're going to provide you with a position that will help you in both areas, and I'm strongly suggesting that you accept it."

I hadn't the foggiest idea of what he was talking about. I had a number of good friends, I was active in my scout troop, Pa trusted me to drive to the farm for our milk every week.

After listening to Mr. Marks tell me I was being offered the job of running the coat check room at the Friday evening dance that paid $5 each evening, I had no trouble deciding to take it. Except for those times when I'd hear the music of some of my favorite popular tunes, like Amapola, and wishing I was on the dance floor, it turned out to be an easy and kind of a fun job – and I liked the money.

Saw in the paper today, that it's the 80th

Art's Odyssey Unplanned

Anniversary of the Keenan Health Center. Located near the 7th district police station off Fond Du Lac Avenue, just north of Burleigh, it was an important site for Harold and I when I was 13.

They'd just come out with a set of 13 shots to immunize against Scarlet Fever, and Ma made sure we got them.

I don't remember if Sis was so privileged or not, but once a week Harold and I walked from 38th and Hampton to 36th and Burleigh to get our shots.

There were some adverse elements involved. Once after a shot we were not to do anything very active, and eat a light meal. Whether it was the long walk or what, but Harold got sicker than a dog after each shot. I didn't.

We had to wait awhile before hiking for home. I usually got my shot first, and while waiting for Harold, the staff gave me the privilege of cleaning equipment; beakers and test tubes in the laboratory adjoining the inoculation room.

Finally, after the 13th shot, we walked home in high spirits. We could finally get as active as our teen bodies would let us! I hadn't got sick, so to celebrate I ate a great meal for supper. The next day, a Saturday, Harold, Kenny Isaacson, and I walked to the Ritz for the afternoon movie.

Toward the end of the 2nd film of the double feature, I began to be concerned. When it ended, I knew I had something to be worried about. I couldn't walk! Harold and Kenny, joining hands, carried me home. My legs were paralyzed! I was scared. Infantile paralysis was rampant at the time, and I was sure I'd become a victim. There was no cure for it, and

I could see myself winding up in an iron lung, or worse, dying too soon.

Once home, Ma got on the phone and called Dr. Morgan. In the course of their conversation, Ma got the message that events had caught up with me, and this was my penalty for getting too active, and eating too much after the last Scarlet Fever shot. The best the good doctor could say was that eventually the paralysis would phase out by itself without any special treatment.

Once I realized that I wasn't a lost cause, and that there was no pain connected with my condition, I could enjoy having to miss school until my legs could work again.

I began delivering an early morning shopping paper, *The 30 Minute Review* when I was 13, I was almost 15 when it began to get interesting. Every Thursday I had to get up at 4:00 a.m. to begin delivering the bundle of *The 30 Minute Review* that had been put on the porch sometime during the night.

One hot summer morning, wearing nothing but short pants, as I was fastening the paper to a screened porch door knob, I noticed a girl sleeping on her back without a stitch on. It took me much longer than usual to fasten the paper.

The next morning was the same, except that her much older sister leaned out of an upstairs window, and as quietly as she could and still be heard made an offer I couldn't refuse. Leaving my shoes outside, I went in a back door and quietly went up the stairs to the second-floor attic.

The older sister's room was at the front of the

house, and she stood in the doorway waving me toward her. Covered in a sheet, she made it clear that she'd drop the sheet when I shed whatever I was wearing.

In a matter of seconds we were both naked, and although one thing led to another, we didn't go all the way. Even though the heat wave continued, delivering the paper to that house became as routine as any other. I never saw anyone there again.

Colder weather brought its own set of problems. To keep the papers in the coaster wagon from blowing away, I put a crowbar on top of the pile.

One morning, a cop came up and asked what I was doing with "the jimmy"? He soon realized I had no idea of what he was talking about, and going to the wagon he lifted the crowbar part way off the papers, realizing why I'd put it there in the first place. It seemed there'd been a break-in in the area and a crowbar had been used.

I found myself fascinated by the transition from night time darkness to the changes in the atmosphere with the rising of the sun. And the increase in traffic and people on the street. My route wasn't that far from two sets of the Milwaukee Road's Railroad tracks.

One going southeast to northwest, and the other almost straight south to north and vice-versa. That was the one that intrigued me with the sounds of cattle heading to the slaughter houses. It was a kind of eerie sensation listening to the low-pitched mooing of those animals with no idea of their fate to be.

Although too young to vote in the 1936 election, I was hoping the Republican candidate Alf Landon from Kansas would beat Roosevelt in the fall election. I thought maybe now we'd have a president from west of the Mississippi River. It didn't happen.

This was also the year Pa, using his soldier's bonus for veterans of World War 1, bought his first new car, a Chev 4 door sedan. I was hoping, because of its historical element, it'd be a Plymouth because the hood ornament on the Plymouth was a small model of the Mayflower.

One summer afternoon, around 3:30 or so, I noticed a larger than usual gray bus heading north on Hopkins Street, suddenly realizing that I'd seen it about the same time every day. Asking Harry Wickman about it, he told me it's the daily bus heading to Mommsen's Hotel.

At supper that evening I asked Pa about "Mommsen's Hotel" eliciting a loud laugh from him. After telling him the source of my knowledge, he told me, "That's one way of putting it, but it's actually the House of Correction run by Mr. Mommsen, and the bus is full of prisoners sentenced to a term there. Then I knew where the bus was going. We'd walked past the prison on Silver Spring Road many times.

Pa, Harold and I listened spell bound to *Cavalcade of America* on the radio on Sunday evenings, and rarely missed hearing *The March of Time* on the radio.

Harold and I, from the small public library on 35th St. just north of Villard Avenue, devoured a series of books by Aldrich, recounting historical fiction of the colonial exploratory and pioneer history of this country. We never missed historically oriented movies like the *Charge of the Light Brigade, Last of the Mohicans,* and *Tale of Two Cities* featuring our first exposure to the guillotine. Some of the women in the relation weren't very happy about Harold and I making models of the guillotine that were used on various insects and worms we found.

In fifth grade I had a teacher named Miss Means. She was anything but! She gave me a dollar to write a poem to go with a present she was giving to a couple at their wedding. It wasn't too long after that when she got married and became Mrs. Evans.

Any kid who could prove that a certain number of non-classroom books had been read, was awarded a big paper certificated testifying to the fact. If everything in school had been that easy, I would have liked school a lot better than I did.

One of the problems I had in Mrs. Evans room was that from my seat I could see the Milwaukee Road railroad tracks only a few blocks east of the school.

I liked watching the switch engines in almost constant movement with the freight cars in that area. My primary interest was the infrequent passenger trains passing through the yards on their way to who knew where, their orange color brightening my day.

That was also the year Ma went in for a tonsillectomy. Pa took us to see her that evening, and I had all I could do not to pass out when I saw her. Not only was she unconscious, but her face and pillow were a bloody mess! Pa got a nurse to take care of things, but we didn't stay.

Leaving St. Anthony's hospital on 10th and State, he took us to the Edgewood Drugstore on Edgewood and Oakland, and treated us to ice cream sundaes; a rare gesture on his part, but he knew we needed something to ease things up for us. I ate my strawberry sundae, but it didn't do much for me.

When King Alexander of Yugoslavia and the Prime Minister of France were assassinated in Marseilles, I was overwhelmed with mixed feelings for the king's young son about my age, losing his father and becoming a king. I worried about whether that was going to start another war as happened when the Crown Prince of Austria was murdered in Sarajevo, Bosnia-Herzegovina in 1914. I didn't know Pa was too old to be drafted if that happened.

Harold and I weren't alone in our interest in geography and history. During high school gym, on a nice day the teacher'd lead us to Smith Park, a couple blocks away to do whatever exercises he had in mind for us. On the way there we'd quiz each other. Someone would name a foreign capital and see who could name the country it was in, or vice-versa. We'd do the same thing matching states and their capital cities. We were too pooped to do the same thing on the walk back.

During my senior year at Custer a group of us lived it up downtown on a Saturday evening. Still going strong after midnight, we caught a dinky at the North Shore station on 6th and Michigan. The dinky was a local streetcar operated by the North Shore Line, running from the station to 5th and Harrison on the south side.

Different from the streetcars operated by the TMRL, it was a four wheeled really short car running on the same rails as the Milwaukee-Chicago trains.

Our group found that by all of us going to the rear of the car and jumping up and down in unison we

Art's Odyssey Unplanned

could actually cause the front end to bounce off the track, stopping the car and making the motorman get out and realign the trolley to the overhead wire. We helped him get the front end back on the track. Doing it once was enough to satisfy our sense of power.

I was thirteen when, with Kenny Isaacson, we found a couple of unopened condoms in the middle of 38th street. Not needing them at the time we walked to Mud Creek and played with them in the water.

A few days later, Ma called me into our bedroom. Doing the wash, she'd found the crumpled dry condom in my pants pocket. It took her an hour of beating around the bush trying to tell me what I already knew about the several reasons men used them.

When fishing the Milwaukee River at Kern Park, we'd often see the police boat, the *Kill Joy* patrolling the water. We didn't know if they did it at night.

Sometimes Werner Harris, a high school classmate and I'd go downtown to take in a movie, have a chocolate malt or sundae afterwards, and then stand on the Wisconsin Avenue bridge and count the condoms we'd see floating down the river. His Dad, from Germany, didn't seem to mind if I was at their house during the day while he was working, and Werner offered me a bottle of his Dad's beer. His Dad was a 6-day bicycle racer fan.

In my junior year, I read an English translation of *Mein Kampf,* Hitler's blue print of the future as he saw it.

After Grandpa Schmitz died, leaving Grandma, Tante Margaret, and Bobby penniless, they moved in with us.

Among things that went to our place was a box of books that Pa'd read when he was a kid. That was my introduction to the stories written by Horatio Alger about poor kids who always made out okay by the end of the book. Their ways of living were almost in direct conflict with ours, so there was a lot of friction.

Ma was a neat and clean housekeeper, and made sure us kids toed the line on doing things like coming in the back door from outside, making sure we didn't track mud or anything in the house. Bobby wouldn't do what we were required to do, making it clear that we weren't his bosses, until Pa put his foot down and Tante Margaret made Bobby do what everyone else had to do. He and I got into some pretty painful heavy hitting scraps as well.

One evening, Bobby and I were alone in my bedroom. We had a heavy metal model of a revolver that happened to be on the floor when he and I got into a fight. He was getting the worst of it because I was using some of the stuff we'd learned when Harold and I practiced boxing with gloves.

That was when he reached down, and before I knew what was happening, he hit me a good solid blow on the side of my head with the gun he'd picked off the floor. It hurt, and made me kind of fuzzy for a bit, but I didn't actually lose consciousness.

I just pretended to do so, scaring the wits out of Bobby who didn't want to get blamed for his action. Harold came in the room just as it happened. He didn't say anything, but later on he'd tease me when I'd goof up by saying something about that being the Bobby effect. Nobody else knew what he was talking about.

I wasn't a student. Homework was only a noun,

Art's Odyssey Unplanned

and grades didn't take that into account. I aced tests and earned exemptions from final exams, but that wasn't enough.

In a conference with my social studies teacher, Ma asked, "Could you tell Arthur to spend more time on his homework and less time on his stamp collection."

Mr. Strutz told her, "His stamps make him the only kid in my class who knows what's going on in the world. He's the only student I have who can spell Czechoslovakia correctly on a quiz, as well as in the native language." I was glad to be there because Ma would never have told me that on her own.

Between sitting for a little kid down the street when his folks went out for an evening, my paper route, a quarter a week allowance, and whatever other money I could scrounge up - I had enough to explore the possibility of a train ride to someplace besides Chicago on a line I'd seen, but never ridden.

When we were small, Pa'd walk Harold and I over to the little North Milwaukee train depot on 34th and Cameron in the early evening. We'd see the Soo Line passenger train coming down the track from the northwest, wondering why we could see the headlight before we could hear the whistle. I loved the bright red color of its coaches.

Sometimes, if I had a spare penny or two, I'd put one on the rail and after the train had passed, pick up a now useless, but flat and stretched out coin to show off at school the next day.

Grandpa Schmitz had run away from his home in Germany at 14 years old, joined the English Navy, jumped ship on the east coast, and managed to get to Milwaukee. Things weren't so great at home for him, so blind though he was, he'd get himself to our house and spend time telling me of his adventures as a sailor.

The first chance I had, I'd tell them to the other kids at school. They loved it, but wound up sticking me with the nickname "Grandpa."

By the time I was in high school, the Soo Line train no longer came through Milwaukee, but I learned that it did stop in Waukesha and found its schedule. One evening I took a Rapid Transit train to Waukesha, and boarded a Soo Line passenger train to Neenah.

I didn't get there until almost midnight, and then found there was no Soo Line train going back to Milwaukee that night. I could see across the river that separated Neenah from Menasha and saw another train station.

Walking across the bridge to Menasha and the depot on the other side, I found there was a Northwestern Railroad train bound for Milwaukee due in an hour or so. It was daylight before I got off that train in Milwaukee, but so early that I had to walk the length of Wisconsin Avenue from the depot near the lake to 8th St. where I waited for a number 20 trolley bus that would take me close to home.

In the spring of 1938, Hitler annexed Austria to his Third Reich, and in autumn took over the Sudetenland of Czechoslovakia.

In Citizenship class I took the affirmative side of a debate on the question as to whether that annexation was justified. Although my personal view was the negative, I simply enjoyed a good argument. I won the debate.

School had barely started in September of 1939

Art's Odyssey Unplanned

when we got the news Germany had moved into Poland and taken the free city of Danzig.

World War II had begun. A few weeks later, my homeroom teacher, Miss Jungton gave me an envelope she'd received from a friend in Germany. The stamps bore the German caption, "Danzig ist Deutsch." Danzig is German.

In May of my senior year, I left my bike at the house as I went to school at the normal time. But after a short walk in the direction of the school, I cut over to Hopkins St. to catch a bus, the first step to going downtown. I boarded a North Shore train for the half hour ride to a local stop in Racine.

It wasn't a long walk to the Horlick Boat and Canoe Livery on the Root River. It had rained the night before, so I was able to negotiate a deal with the woman in charge. In return for emptying all the boats and canoes I could have a canoe free for the rest of the day. I'd come prepared with a lunch in a paper bag and a thermos of coffee.

I paddled some distance up stream to a small island and went skinny dipping for a while. There's something about going through water touching every inch of skin unencumbered by anything else. Combining lunch with a bit of sunbathing, eventually I paddled back, returning the canoe in time to catch a train back to Milwaukee, and home about the same time as I usually did.

Sis, now a freshman in our very small high school, had noticed my absence, and in return for her promise not to tell, got the whole story. Her comment was simple. "You're not gonna get away with stuff like that in the army."

Art Schmitz

Pa was an officer in the Woodmen of the World, a fraternal organization that included most of his friends from his pre-war days. They usually met at the Bohemian Hall on 12th and Reservoir, which was also the scene of their annual Christmas party.

At the Christmas party, a lot of the kids would recite Christmas poems and stories, and there'd be singing of Christmas Carols. Some kids would play piano pieces, or do short Christmas plays.

Most of the musicians weren't, in my opinion, very good. I'd heard too much professional music on the radio and records. The highlight of the evening of course was handing out gift bags for each kid at the party. The bags were big and loaded with all kinds of good candies, nuts, small toys, etc.

I'd had a little difference of opinion with another kid when I was in 4th grade. We'd both been sent to the office and were read the riot act about our behavior. I was still in a blue funk when I walked in our back yard. Elmer, cousin Dorothy's husband was there. Looking at me, he said, "Boyce, you were in trouble again at school!" I thought he was psychic or something, wondering to myself "How did he know?" Worse yet, I thought if Ma and Pa knew, I wouldn't be allowed to go to the Woodmen's party that evening. Luckily, Elmer didn't say anything, so I had a really great time that evening.

One evening when Grandma Schmitz was living with us, she saw me doing something with my stamp collection. "Boyce" she said, "Why you waste your time with little pieces of paper." "Grandma", I said, "Maybe someday I'll go to the places these stamps came from." "Ach, Boyce, Das ist fur die Millionaren."

Art's Odyssey Unplanned

One day I said I was going to the library. Grandma asked me, "Ach Boyce, will you bring me back some romance books?" Although I understood some German, I had no idea of what titles to look for in the fairly decent assortment of German books on the shelves, so I picked a few at random.

A couple of them, I guess, were what Grandma wanted. But, a few evenings later, Pa was sprawled out resting on the davenport in the parlor. I was listening to something on the radio and Grandma was sitting reading one of the books I brought for her. All of a sudden, she got up fast, threw the book she'd been reading across the room, and stomped to her bedroom.

Pa was laughing when I asked, "What was that all about?" He stopped laughing long enough to tell me I'd brought Grandma, Eric Remarque's novel *All Quiet on the Western Front*, and Grandma'd got to the part where Germany was losing the war.

I loved the switch from the 35th St. grade school to Custer High School. For one thing, there was, at least in the minds of the staff at each school, an orientation day when we were marched from our grade school to the high school.

We spent the better part of an afternoon in the high school building, getting a tour of the various elements of high school; the gym, boys locker room, industrial ed shops, class rooms, study hall, library, and topped off with a concert by the high school band in their striking uniforms - red tunics and white pants.

I looked forward to the idea of going to a different room and teacher for each subject. The first week was sheer novelty, topped off with a pep rally on Friday, shortening some of the class periods.

But, starting on the second Monday, reality set in. I didn't have too much of a problem with my other classes, but the required arithmetic class was sheer agony.

In the lower grades, I'd managed to master multiplication problems and simple long division, but now I was expected to master long division with multiple digits for divisors and remainders, and it wasn't working for me. I'd never got high grades in arithmetic, but now they were well below passing.

Up until now I'd been satisfied with a passing grade, if not high marks, but flunking was more than depressing, and that was what was happening. I wasn't really afraid of her, but I just couldn't ask Mrs. Bennett for help. To me at least, she seemed something less than human, never smiling or showing any sign of interest in anything but the subject at hand. Her efforts at explaining the procedures went over my head.

When things got really bad, I'd console myself with comparing my situation to the Verdun attack by the German Army in World War I. I paraphrased Marshall Foch's comment "They shall not pass," to "This too will pass."

Taking a shortcut on the way home after school, I'd walk through an alley. About a block north of our house, I saw a beautiful Scotch Collie in a wire fenced yard. I started to kneel on the alley side of the fence, and the dog would come over to have its ears scratched.

It wasn't long before I started to pour out my

troubles to the dog, who I was certain understood every word. Finally, leaving the dog, I was able to go on home with a lighter heart and enjoy the rest of the day.

I was 12 when one wintry day I walked up the alley on my way to Sunday School at Trinity Lutheran Church on 37th Street, a few blocks north of our house. My foot hit an icy spot and I fell on my knees. It didn't really hurt until later in the day.

The next day Pa and Ma took me to Doctor Morgan's office. Looking at my knee, he told us I had an abscess, and he'd have to lance it.

Always shy of being stuck with needles, I'd pass out when we got shots or vaccinations at school. The shots at school were against Diphtheria, Smallpox, and Whooping Cough. I don't know what it was for, but there was one called a Schick test. That one I didn't mind. Anyway, I rebelled.

Even after the folks agreed to buy me a big package of stamps from all over the world that I'd seen in a store window, I couldn't give in. In desperation, they forced me to lay down on the table so Doctor Morgan could lance my knee. I struggled and yelled out and Pa passed out on top of me.

About that time, Dr. Morgan gave us the word. In my struggles, the abscess had opened up and he didn't have to lance the knee. I still got my stamp package.

For some years we'd been getting our milk from a farm out on Hampton Avenue. Pa usually took Harold and I along to the Grant farm. I got some kind of a kick out of watching the numbers change on the odometer as we drove along. One day Ma went along and decided things weren't sanitary enough.

She learned that a relative of a couple living with us had a farm way out on Hopkins street, and after checking it out decided that's where we'd get our milk. Not too long after I'd got my driver's license, Pa'd have me take the five-gallon can out to get the milk.

I'd take a few detours before getting out to the farm, but always came straight back after getting the milk.

Once, on the way back, I was distracted by something and had to make a quick swerve back to the right lane of the road, causing the can in front of the right front seat to suddenly tip.

With frightening visions of what would be said if I got home with a spilled can, with my left hand on the wheel, I made a quick grab with my right and managed to keep the milk from spilling. Relieved at the knowledge that I wouldn't be deprived of being the milk delivery man, I eased my way home.

I enjoyed an extra benefit from the farm milk. Ma'd put it in glass milk bottles and let it sit for a time. The cream would rise to the top and Ma would whip it up to use it in her homemade cream puff shells. Talk about rich and sweet!

I was about nine one Sunday evening. The grownups were in the parlor, and Harold, Sis, Bobby and I were in the boy's bedroom trying to figure out something to do.

I got an idea. I put a hassock on top of the chifforette, and a grape basket on top of that. Then, climbing up to the top of the chifforette, I figured if I got on top of the grape basket I could touch the ceiling. So, sitting on the grape basket I reached up, but before I could touch the ceiling, the grape basket broke and the next thing I knew was the sensation of watching the room swirl around me as everything fell to the floor.

I wound up sitting on the hassock none the worse for wear, but thrilled at the exciting sights of the room as I fell. It must have made some noise, because seconds after I landed, the grownups barged into the room to see us calmly doing not much of anything, and me sitting sedately on the hassock.

I don't really know why I often spent weekends at Grandma and Grandpa Bakers place, but I didn't mind.

I always enjoyed the bus and streetcar ride, especially the number 15 streetcar on the last leg of the long ride down there. I always hoped, and often was rewarded with having to wait for a coal boat to pass under the open Water Street bridge.

Their cottage was heated with a couple of coal stoves that gave off a cheery glow through the eisenglass windows on the front door, that also doubled as the entry for adding more coal when needed. Grandpa had been seriously hurt when the horses he'd been driving had bolted in traffic, so Grandma did a lot of things by herself.

Money was short, but even if it wasn't, Grandma wouldn't spend a cent if she could get it for free, and coal was one of those things. I'd pull the coaster wagon when we walked along some railroad tracks in the area, and she'd scrounge for coal found next to the tracks from the steam locomotives passing through.

I always enjoyed walking to the big Goodwill store

on 6th and National with Grandma. It was a long walk, but no matter what the weather, if Grandma wanted to go to the Goodwill store, we went. Grandpa Baker always stayed home.

Getting to the store, we'd go to the top floor and eyeball all the merchandise as we worked our way down to the street level. Grandma never had anything special in mind, but if she saw something she thought she could use, she bought it for a lot less than the same thing would cost anywhere else. I just liked looking at the variety of things in the store, but if I saw something I liked, and said so, Grandma became totally deaf.

Shortly after Grandpa Baker died, arrangements were made for Grandma to move in with us. A room had been built for her in our attic, and heating had been worked into it so she'd be okay in cold weather.

Ma'd hired the farmer who supplied us with milk to move Grandma's stuff. I don't know where Harold and Sis were farmed out while the move was made, but I was sent to stay with Ruth Seerup and her mother during the days that it took.

I probably drove them crazy with questions about all kinds of things, like a picture of Ruth's brother Carl in uniform. I knew Carl worked for the Milwaukee Road Railroad at their roundhouse below the 27th St. viaduct.

I knew better than to tell Ruth I thought she was a liar when she told me, "Carl said his time in the army were the happiest days of his life." He'd been in the World War, and I couldn't believe that anyone could be happy getting shot at.

She had another brother, Norman. He was more

cheerful than Carl when we visited, but wound up in the County Sanitarium in Wauwatosa. We visited him there once, and he wasn't as cheerful as he'd been before. I didn't know what they meant when it was said that he'd been committed because he liked young boys. So, what was wrong with that?

Ma paid regular visits to the Seerup's home when Mrs. Seerup was sick and took us kids along. Mrs. Seerup, a white haired old lady was usually lying down on a couch in the living room.

We were visiting when she asked Ruth to get it. Ruth came back with a pan, and Mrs. Seerup vomited some yellow stuff into the pan that Ruth took away. It was less than a week later that we went to see Mrs. Seerup laid out at the Voth and Anderson Funeral Home on National Avenue. She'd had stomach cancer.

Sis was the conscientious one of us kids, so was often embarrassed by Harold or I, but more so with me.

Mrs. Mais, her girlfriend Wanny's mother, was the direct opposite of her father, who didn't have much use for us guys. Wanny was her nickname, and a lot easier to say than her real name.

When Mrs. Mais had their car, she'd take us kids to places like Waukesha Beach, an amusement park in the next county when it had penny days. One nice summer day she took us to Silver Spring park for a picnic on the grass. It was great!

She'd brought along everything needed for a picnic lunch. Soft drinks, buns, hot dogs, etc. I loved it. There was plenty for everybody, and I enjoyed my share of hot dogs with ketchup on the buns.

But, when we got home, Ma got an earful from Sis. She'd been so embarrassed because I'd eaten 13 hot dogs! I think she was the only one counting, because when I'd ask Mrs. Mais for another one, I got it.

One Saturday afternoon, Harold, Sis, me, Kenny Isaacson, and Wanny, walked to the Ritz theater on Villard Avenue and started talking about what our parents did for punishment if they thought we needed it.

Harold, Sis, and I weren't happy about listening to our folks harping on what they thought were our misdeeds. Wanny said she'd prefer that to not being talked to at all for more than a week, while Kenny told us his Dad would simply use his belt on his butt. Before reaching the theater, except for Kenny, we agreed that we'd prefer his Dad's belt and get it over with.

As upper classmen, Harold and I were party guys. It was going on midnight when we got home one evening.

Seeing Sis, with books and papers sprawled out on the dining room table, we asked her, "Sis, why knock yourself out with all that stuff and have some fun some evening?" She said, "Well, somebody has to vindicate the honor of this family!" She went on to become the valedictorian of her class.

Pa let me have the car one great summer evening. A couple of friends chipped in a quarter a piece to fill the tank with gas at 15 cents a gallon. After some cruising around, we stopped at a restaurant on east Capitol Drive in Shorewood. We all wore clean slacks and sport shirts.

Art's Odyssey Unplanned

After a half hour or so of waiting to be served when we saw people who'd come in after us being served, we walked out. It turned out that our offense was not wearing suit coats. We wound up at Shorty's on Villard Avenue where we could have been wearing overalls and been served.

One late fall Sunday afternoon, we were at Grandma Schmitz's house on North 8th street. Not interested in the gabbing of the grownups, I asked Pa if we could have the car for a while. Giving me the keys, he said "Just be back by suppertime."

Harold, Sis, Bobby, and I took off. With no special place in mind I drove up to Lincoln Park to see that a new bridge had been built over the Milwaukee River. Even though the road to it hadn't been paved I drove to the west end of the bridge.

We got within a few feet of the bridge to realize we weren't going to get there very easy. The car got stuck in the mud. I tried to ease it out by slowly accelerating the engine forward, and then backward with no progress at all. Now what do we do!

Harold and Bobby got out and tried pushing the front of the car while I used the motor without success. Now our worries got serious as we wondered if we were going to get back as ordered.

Finally, noticing some planks alongside the road, we slid them under the rear wheels and, like wow, it worked. I was able to get the car back on solid ground!

Satisfied to be able to get going again, we still had the problem of getting back with the car as clean as it had been when we left. Driving to our house, we got a bucket from the basement, and using water from the outside tap for the hose, we managed to get the car relatively clean again in just about enough time to get back to 8th St. in time for supper.

The following week, with the weather getting worse, Pa let me have the car so he wouldn't have to run some errands for Ma. That Chev sometimes had problems with choking the motor. Of course, it could never be the drivers fault.

I'd taken care of most of the errands, when I decided I'd have time to go to our library. After leaving the library with several books, I got in the car, and turned the ignition key. There was a soft growl, but no ignition.

Bundling up, I got the crank out of the trunk, stuck it in the opening under the grill, and cranked and cranked and cranked; working up a real sweat. Just before I was about to go back in the library to ask if I could use their phone to call home, I got her going, then hopped back into the car, fed it some gas, and pulled away for home. The rest of the errands didn't get done that day.

I always liked to sing. Pa belonged to a couple of organizations that used small song books at their meetings, and he'd always bring one home for me.

Most of the songs were those I'd hear on the radio, so I had no trouble knowing the melody without the notes. And at home, I'd sing those songs whenever I felt like it, which was often.

One day Harold squawked to Ma, "Ma, make him stop that singing." Ma told him, "I'd rather hear that than his crying."

Although no one in our relation played a musical instrument, music was a big part of life, no matter what the occasion. Besides the Christmas songs, some of them for us in German, there were the folk and popular songs on the radio - and for our very German family, the Irish tunes for St. Patrick's Day that we celebrated, especially after Prohibition was repealed, with green beer.

Pa never passed up anything that was free, and there was a lot of it. Getting to it was never a problem, even if it meant taking five different buses and streetcars to the other end of town. We often went to Humboldt Park on the far south side to see events like Gilbert and Sullivan's *Pirates of Penzance,* exposing me to the first performance of classical music.

In school, during music appreciation class, we were obligated to write stuff about the composer and the music while listening to pieces like Schubert's *March Militaire.* I was too busy listening to do any writing, and didn't worry about any effects on my grade.

It didn't take long for me to realize that the theme song for the Lone Ranger on the radio was from Rossini's *William Tell Overture.* Not long after getting my own Victrola, I learned that I could buy green label classical music records downtown for 29 cents.

One evening after I'd got my driver's license, Pa had me put the car in the garage across the alley. He paid them $5 a month for that.

I'd got the front end in when for some weird reason, I choked the motor and didn't hit the brake fast enough as the car rolled back, the right front bumper catching on the edge of the door, tearing it partly off.

For a split second, I knew I was in trouble, but seeing Pa angrily jumping up and down like a jumping jack in the alley was just too funny to me. I waited a few minutes to stop laughing before I got out of the car. Pa calmed down a bit, and told me to give it another try, and this time I'd better get it in without doing more damage. This time I got it in okay.

After Grandpa Schmitz died, Grandma, Tante Margaret, and Bobby moved in with us. Among the things that went to our place was a box of books that Pa had read when he was a kid. That was my introduction to the stories written by Horatio Alger about poor kids who always made out okay by the end of the book.

I was 16 when my cousin Ken Peterson got married. His wife, Lydia was from a Polish family, so the wedding celebration was a long one that ran into the wee hours of the next day. It was almost midnight, with the music and dancing still going on, when the food was put out.

The food was mostly traditional Milwaukee celebratory eats. Besides the wedding cake, there was a great variety of other dessert dishes, but there was also a Milwaukee standard - cannibal sandwiches. That is raw ground beef on rye bread, with salt and onions, potato salad, coffee, beer, etc. I ate and ate and ate, and drank my share of soft drinks.

After a while, I went outside to a warm, quiet night. Next to the outer wall of the hall, there was a large container that turned out to be a good place to sit on and rest. Around 3 o'clock the next morning I woke up and went back in to eat some more. The sun had come up before we went home.

Art's Odyssey Unplanned

One fall weekend, Harold and I rode to Chicago with Jack Gehl in his old Ford. As usual, I had a good time down there. On our early way back to Milwaukee on Highway 41, we got as far as Glencoe, Illinois when the car conked out. Traffic was still light, so Harold and I pushed it across the two lanes to the driveway of a closed filling station on the west side of the highway.

Walking back to the northbound lane of the highway, we started trying to hitch a ride back home. Finally, a guy driving an almost new Cord stopped to give us a lift. Jack rode in the right front seat, with Harold and I in the back seat. In Wisconsin, there was no state speed limit at that time, so we could see that the guy was going 90mph!

We listened to the guy telling about his work as an agent for the FBI, laughing to ourselves as we leafed through his liquor sales catalogs on the back seat. He took us right up to our house, and we were only a half-hour late for school.

That evening, Pa drove us back to Glencoe. There, tying a rope to our 36 Chev and the other end to Jack's car, Pa towed the Ford. I was assigned to steer the Ford so there'd be no danger of it swerving into oncoming traffic. I wasn't crazy about doing it, but didn't feel I had a choice. Every mile was a strain as I tried to make sure I was doing the right thing to keep the Ford as aligned as I could with Pa's Chev, but we got back home okay.

There were times during summer vacation when Jack Gehl would drive Harold, Sis, Rita, and I to the Riverview amusement park. It had rides I'd never seen before, the prices were reasonable, so until we had to meet Jack at the gate at a pre-set time we'd have the time of our lives going in circles, up and down, or shooting down a slippery slide.

Our whole family was in Chicago for Labor Day with Bobby along this time. The weather was too nice for us to sit in the house listening to the grownups chew the fat, so we headed out for some fun. For whatever reason, Sis wasn't with us.

Taking the Irving Park streetcar to Sheridan Road, we transferred to a double deck bus heading south. We got off and walked east, crossing Michigan Ave. over to the Shedd Aquarium, and the Planetarium. We didn't have the money to go to it, but we knew there was some kind of rodeo going on at Soldiers Field.

We were just on the south side of the Planetarium when we saw a lot of cops not that far away. Through a speaker cone we got the word they were there because a live bull that was part of the rodeo show had escaped and we should get out of the area we were in.

It only took a minute for us to realize that the closest escape route was to climb up the wall on our side of the Planetarium. Being the gentlemen we were, we helped Rita go up first. To do that, she had to get up on my shoulder from where she could reach up, and with some help from us pushing her feet up, she could make it. Her only concern was that we wouldn't look up at her from our lower position. We promised, but she couldn't see our fingers crossed. I was the last guy left, so after everyone else was up, I made a quick run up the hill to the front entrance of the Planetarium.

Sometimes, going home after a visit to the bakery on Villard Ave., my friend, Eddy Chesnik would let me ride on his bike with him. One day, as we rode home he said, "Schmitz, I don't understand you, but I like you anyway."

During the depression of the 30's, Milwaukee set up a system of what were called Social Centers. Most of them were in schools, but some were in places like the old North Milwaukee Fire House. They offered a variety of different classes, like chess clubs, where the city paid nominal fees to men and women who were experts in their fields. Ma was proud to know that one of her favorite teachers, Dorothy Endris was heading that program.

I was 12 or 13 when I got involved in the chess class at the old firehouse. I was getting pretty good at it, and it went to my head a bit. I got put down good after telling some other kids "I'm more refined and cultured than you are."

On a spring Saturday after my 14th birthday, Ma asked me to dig up part of the back yard for the garden she was going to plant. Her specialty was gladiolus.

It was one of those comfortably warm days, with just a hint of a breeze when I first put the shovel into the fairly soft ground and dug up a chunk of dirt. Actually, it was kind of fun.

I didn't pay too much attention to it at first, but as I dug up more ground, I noticed a number of night crawlers moving out of the dirt I'd dug up. I dug some more dirt before putting the shovel down, getting an empty tin can, and picking up the worms to put in the can with some dirt.

I didn't go in the house to tell anyone, but went down to the basement, picked up a cane pole already geared up with a line, bobber, and hook, and an empty burlap bag and started hiking east to the Milwaukee River. It didn't take long before I'd caught my first Bullhead, followed by several more to put in the bag.

Pa'd warned us to be careful handling Bullheads because of their stinging capabilities. What he didn't tell us was that it wasn't those tentacle like projections on their face that did the stinging. I learned the hard way that it was the spines in their fins on the back that kept me awake most of that night.

The fish weren't small, and weighted down by the bag, it took me longer to walk home than it did to get to the river. It was supper time before I got there, so the fish went into the fridge until after supper. Pa agreed to clean them if I'd finish the garden digging job while he did so. We had fish for supper the next day.

At 14, with a crush on Sis's friend Betty Koshnick, who lived up the street from us, I enrolled in the same religious instruction class they were in.

Ma belonged to Die Neue Apostolische Kirche, the New Apostolic Church, and Pa didn't go to any church, so we were free to choose. The instruction class was at Atonement Lutheran Church on 42nd and Ruby, and run by Pastor Schaefer. My friend Jack Langtry was also going there. Another attraction was getting out of school early to attend a religious element.

I didn't immediately realize that I was also going to be giving up a Saturday morning every week- along

Art's Odyssey Unplanned

with the Tuesday and Thursday hours of instruction, plus having to memorize bible passages, etc. We were also expected to attend Sunday School and the service immediately after that.

Once, after Sunday School, Jack and I were heading over to his house just up the street from the church when Pastor Schaefer came out of the parsonage heading to the church for the service. Seeing us, he knew we weren't going to be in church, so pointing at us, he solemnly declared "Fools go where angels fear to tread."

My problem memorizing prose reared up its ugly head at the end of the two years of instructions. Examinations evening was held the Thursday before Confirmation on Sunday. That evening we were going to be examined by Pastor Schaefer in front of the congregation. I was really terrified, but couldn't think of any way to avoid it. So, standing in front of the congregation with all the other kids, I awaited my fate.

One by one, Pastor asked each kid to recite a Bible passage to illustrate a point. I stopped breathing for a minute when, calling my name, he asked me to explain an item from scripture! Stunned for a moment at the realization that he understood my problem and was giving me an out, I did as he asked. Although we'd had our differences in class during the last two years, I loved the man.

None of the jobs I'd had since graduation from high school were satisfying in any way, so when I heard about a government program called the NYA, or National Youth Administration, I looked into it. From early on, I'd been interested in planes, and working under the NYA I'd be involved in learning Aircraft Maintenance.

With my bum right eye, I doubted I'd ever be able to get a pilot's license, but this would at least get me involved with aircraft. I applied and was accepted. At that point in time, I think they'd have accepted almost anyone.

Now I had to get up at 5 a.m. to be able to get to the County Airport by 8 a.m., and it only paid $6.00 a week, but that was better than nothing if I'd wind up getting a real paying job servicing airplanes.

There were several other guys in our small group under the direction of Mr. Doerflinger working in a hangar on the east side of the airport. One of them, Sheridan Dreyer, didn't live too far from me, so we usually played cards on the streetcar on the way out, and often on the way home. We got to be good friends, and I spent a lot of pleasant evenings at his house, often playing cards while listening to his immense collection of classical music records.

The kicker was that we had to walk the mile or so from Bolivar, the south end of the #11 streetcar line to the airport. Sometimes, if we were lucky, we'd get a ride from one of the other guys who had a car and happened to be there when we got off the streetcar.

His car was an older model Ford with a rumble seat, and sometimes we would get a ride with him to the end of the streetcar line. One day, one of the guys stepped off the car while it was still moving and with no problem, ran to get the streetcar standing there.

A few days later, seeing the same situation, I did the same thing but not with the same result. My feet hit the pavement and I went tail over tea kettle, finally crawling to the curb. Sitting down and leaning against a telephone pole it took over an hour before I felt I could get on a streetcar.

By the time I got home, I felt a lot better. But later that evening my right arm was killing me, so I called Dr. Morgan who suggested I take a couple of aspirin and come in the next morning. Instead of going to work, I headed to his office the next day. After some x-rays, he told me I had a cracked, but not broken, elbow and fitted me with a sling for the arm that I was to wear for 3 weeks.

I was back at the hangar the next day, wearing the sling, but still able to do whatever I had to do. Because of the war, instead of learning the ins and outs of aircraft maintenance, we were putting Air Corps insignia on DC-3's being converted to C-47's.

About a week after my accident, Jack Langtry biked over one hot evening and asked if I wanted to go swimming. Tossing the sling in our closet, I got on my bike and we headed for Kletch Park on the river for an evening of skinny dipping. I never wore the sling again.

Often, the guy with the car would take a bunch of us to the Oak Creek Power Plant east of the airport. Then we'd take a streetcar that was supposed to be for the men who worked there, to the east end of the line. From there we'd walk to the top of the bluff above the lake to a spot where there was a sloping area that we used to slide down to the narrow beach at the bottom. There we'd strip and wade into the water toward a huge flat topped rock, it's upper surface just a foot or so below the surface.

From there we'd dive into the water and swim around for a while. The fun part was climbing back up the bluff when we were ready to head for home.

My friend Sheridan was as nice a guy as there was, but he was also as naïve as they come. One really hot day, one of the guys handed him an empty can with a seal at the top and told him to walk over to the Army Reserve unit on the west side of the airport and ask them to fill the can with prop wash. Planes had props, right? And sometimes they needed washing, right?

It took Sheridan most of the morning to cross the entire airport, but he got back in a hurry. A full Colonel drove him back in a jeep, had Mr. Doerflinger assemble our group, and read us the riot act about wasting manpower in a wartime setting. Sheridan learned that prop wash was the term given to the air flow generated by a planes propeller in flight.

I became acutely aware that I wasn't really learning anything, and even more so that I needed more money as well as easier hours. I landed a job as a produce dispatcher at the National Tea Company warehouse on Jackson Street.

I started work at 8 p.m. and finished at 4 a.m. the next morning. The work was an easy, mostly sitting down thing. Pa let me use the car to get to and from work, as long as I got home before he needed it to get to work.

I thought I was pretty much with it, until I heard the mostly much older guys at work talking about their off-time experiences. Most had never gone to high school, so their language was pretty earthy as they talked about the women they'd had, where they met, and what they did - described in graphic detail.

I kept in touch with Norman Panas, one of the guys at the NYA, and we often double dated, Pa letting me have the car. Norm lived in Cudahy, so it was a long drive across town to get to his place.

One day after one of those dates, Pa didn't get home at the usual time, Ma worrying herself sick over it. He finally got home in time for supper, and before changing out of his mailman's uniform tore into me with both barrels.

It seems there wasn't enough gas in the tank for him to start the car that morning so he had to take the bus to get to work, and being late as a result. After supper, he said "How in the world did you manage to get the car in the garage on the last gas in the tank?" After that we agreed that whoever had the car had to leave at least a quarter tank of gas in the tank. I walked to the nearest filling station to get a gallon of gas, enough to drive over and fill the tank.

As a freshman, I took general science as an elective. Mr. Cinkosky was the teacher, and not only knew his subject, but kids as well. His assignments weren't always that easy, but they were always stuff I could do.

He only said it once, but it stuck. "Ignorance is knowing too much that ain't so." Imagine! A teacher talking in the vernacular!

To become more thoroughly immersed in science, I spent a lot of my spare time in his room cleaning test tubes and other laboratory equipment.

Shortly after discovering the Scott Stamp catalog, I got the idea to start a stamp club at school. To have a club of any kind required getting a teacher to agree to be a sponsor. I asked Miss Allen, my English teacher if she'd be the sponsor. She agreed to do so, and said we could use her room after school on Tuesday.

It didn't take long before we had quite a number of kids coming to the meetings and sharing their particular interests where postage stamps were concerned.

With the way things were going in Asia and Europe, there was a lot of interest in the stamps of countries in those areas. It turned out that the club continued for several years after I graduated.

In one of my frequent meetings with Mr. Marks, it took real effort to keep from laughing out loud in front of him. That's all he would have needed. He said, "Schmitz, I think a big part of your problem is that you're not getting enough physical exercise." As I restrained my impulse to laugh, I thought of Mr. Cinkosky's definition of ignorance.

I was entranced with anything to do with water, especially boats. I had a fairly large toy sailboat that I sometimes kept in my locker. After school, I'd walk over to the lagoon at Silver Spring Park to sail it. I'd figured out how to set the sails and the rudder so it would sail to the other side of the lagoon, depending on which way the wind was blowing, or so that it would sail in a kind of semi-circle and sail back to where I started it.

School let out at 3:15, but between the times I was at the park or just biking around for the fun of it, I rarely got home much before supper.

We would have taken our bikes to high school, but there was no place to put them while we'd be in class, so we walked. Pa had some mailman friends

Art's Odyssey Unplanned

in different post offices, and Harold and I knew them all. One cold wintry day we were walking to school when a parcel post truck stopped at the curb. Driving it was Dewey Plauman, who invited us to get in the other side of his truck, and drove us the rest of the way to the school.

I hit on every kid I knew on the Student Council to see if we could get the school to set up a bike rack somewhere on the grounds, so those of us who could bike would have a place to store our bikes while in class.

There was a lot of discussion, signing petitions, etc., but when Mr. Weingartner didn't want something, it didn't happen. So much for democracy.

In chemistry I got to know a kid living near school, Ed Hoffman. He'd often come to my place after school, or I'd go to his. For Christmas I'd got a microscope, slides, and some stuff to look at, and we'd play around with that.

At his place one day, we went down to his basement. He'd swiped a pack of his Dad's Lucky Strike's and we lit up and smoked. It felt pretty neat and grown up, so we had to do another.

After finishing that, I headed out. Instead of going home I walked to Silver Spring Park. The further I walked, the worse I felt. Getting to the park, I sat down leaning my back on a tree. Man, was I woozy! It seemed to take forever before I felt I could stand up to say nothing of being able to walk again. Finally, after I don't know how long, I was able to stand up and walk home with a clear head again.

During recess at the 35th St. School, I was sitting on a basement window sill browsing through a small booklet with incredibly beautiful colored pictures of birds.

All of a sudden, Kenny Lengling came up, pulled the booklet out of my hands and tore it in half. I was too stunned to do anything about it so I just sat and wondered why anyone would do anything like that.

In 7th grade I became a Cabbage Head. That was what we called the kids who became Safety Cadets that acted as crossing guards at intersections around the school.

Besides having some clout over the other kids, like reporting them for refusal to wait if we stopped them because of traffic, we got to wear a large yellow emblem on our arm.

The next year I became a Cream Puff, that is, a Captain responsible for supervising a number of Cabbage Heads. One of them was Kenny Lengling. I asked him if he'd meet with me at our house to go over some corner assignments I was considering.

He came over after school one day, and while we were talking things over, Ma brought us some milk and homemade cookies. Kenny got the strangest look on his face and I asked if he felt okay. I was stunned! Kenny, an 8th grader like me, broke down crying his heart out.

Too surprised to say anything, I sat there and waited for him to stop crying. It took a while, but he finally regained his composure. "Art," he said between sobs, "I'm so sorry I tore your book that time, and here you are, and your mother, treating me like the human being that I never get at home. From here on out, I'll do anything you say I should do as a Cabbage Head."

Art's Odyssey Unplanned

I'd never thought about how good a home I had, and Kenny wasn't the only one.

Walking to and from Manual Training with Alex Sinner, Alex told me, "I wish I'd never been born." I didn't ask him why, but figured his home life must be miserable to make a kid feel that way.

Herbert Schuster, another classmate who lived on 37th St. just south of Stark, and I often spent time at each other's houses. His folks had come over from Austria, and his mother, for whatever reason, liked me and often offered me absolutely delicious homemade bakery. Herb was with me when Ma and I had a small difference of opinion about something. Walking to his house afterwards, he said, "If I ever talked to my Ma like that, she'd hit me on the head."

Gym was on the bottom of the list of favorite subjects. Between not being as well coordinated as most of the other guys, and the vision problem with my right eye, I was always the last guy to be picked for a team.

The one exception was volleyball where I did pretty well. The other was the rope climbing thing. Being a light weight and not fearing heights, I had no problem climbing the rope to the very top where, using my feet to keep a grip on the rope, I'd grab the metal girder at the ceiling and yell down to any of my pals on the floor. I'd often stay up there till Mr. Wulk, the teacher, would order me to descend.

Except for its interference with sports like baseball, the eye thing bothered Ma and Pa more than it did me. I overheard them talking once, and Pa said, "There's nothing wrong with his eyes. When we were at the lake the other day, he could see a ship that was almost on the horizon just as well as I could."

Ma took me to an eye doctor, who told her I'd never be able to drive a car with an eye like that. She got me enrolled in some kind of eye sight training program at Marquette University.

The most interesting feature for me there, was being able to tour their Pathology Museum while waiting my turn. I didn't know it at the time but their Vision Department offered to surgically straighten my right eye without charge. Scared stiff of any kind of surgery, Ma turned it down.

The next step was having me go to an office near 3rd and North Avenue after school where I was hooked up to a machine that was supposed to condition my eyes to work together. Being painless, and giving me another place to go, I didn't mind.

While waiting my turn, I got to know another kid pretty well, to the point where he invited me to his place after I was through. I wound up going there often because his sister and I got along real good. A dark-haired beauty the same age as I was, we shared a lot of the same interests - music, reading, and going places.

I'd come to realize I needed a larger stamp album, so bought a red, hard cover Modern Stamp Album, which meant hours of moving stamps from my original soft cover Ivory Soap Album. Somehow or other, I found out about a couple of stamp companies that would send me approvals, that is, small sheets or glassine envelopes of stamps that I could buy, sending by return mail the money for those I kept and returning those I didn't want.

Art's Odyssey Unplanned

One of those was Charles Cleveland in a Chicago suburb. He offered a deal where by buying a certain amount, I'd get a nice item for free.

Harold also had a decent collection. One day he needed some money for something else he wanted and asked me if I'd be interested in buying his collection.

I said, "I'll give you 75 cents for it." He agreed, and I became the proud owner of a New Zealand stamp he had that I knew was worth ten times that much from my perusal of Scott's Stamp Catalog.

On a nice day, I sometimes liked to use my magnifying glass for something other than looking at stamps. It became a source of revenue after some kids saw me burning small pieces of paper on the steps of the high school. I bought several for 5 cents each at the dime store on Villard Avenue, and sold them to other kids for 10 cents.

Sometimes during lunch hour I'd go to the little store on 36th Street across from the school. I could buy a small pie for 10 cents and take it back with me to the auditorium where I'd be for my next class, the School Chorus.

The pie would be on a small light cardboard plate. Once, being a little late, I didn't finish eating the pie till class had begun. Finished with the pie, I licked off any residue from the plate, and didn't quite know what to do with it. Seeing a friend over on the other side of the auditorium, I flipped it over to him. He saw it coming, grabbed it and sent it back to me the same way. Mr. Boldt, the teacher, wasn't thrilled and gave both of us an after school detention.

Later that semester, the music department

scheduled a program for the public. Thanks to records I had at home, I was familiar with the chorus from *Aida* and the *Anvil Chorus*, both to be sung at the program with some interesting changes in the libretto in the chorus from *Aida*.

For the *Anvil Chorus* a couple of the kids in the percussion section of the orchestra were going to be hammering on real anvils! We in the chorus asked Mr. Boldt if we could sing "You Are My Sunshine." We got a very definite "NO" from him.

The Auditorium was packed with parents, relatives, and friends the night of the concert. We were prepped up for it as well. The music and vocals went off in perfection till we got to the *Anvil Chorus*.

When Mr. Boldt brought the baton down to begin, the orchestra and chorus broke into "You Are My Sunshine." Somehow or other, the kids in the orchestra had got hold of the music for the piece. We in the Chorus knew the melody and words by heart.

Mr. Boldt got so red in his face I thought he'd have a stroke, but continued until the end of the piece. Even he smiled as the audience stood up, applauded, and yelled out for several minutes before sitting down again. We still got D's on our report cards.

After graduation, I worked one of my jobs for a whole 45 minutes. It was a small company on 27th Street and Auer Avenue. It had a contract to make signal lanterns for the Navy. Assembly began on the first floor and the finished lanterns were packaged on the third floor. My job was to carry the cardboard flats that became the cartons from the basement to the third floor. There was no elevator. After 45

Art's Odyssey Unplanned

minutes, I walked out the door instead of going down for another load.

I'd joined the YMCA at its building on 4th Street just south of Wisconsin Ave. mainly to swim. It was a men's only club, so suits were never used. I got along with a guy I met there, Wesley Koby. We'd heard that Gracie Fields, an English comedienne, had a radio program on a Chicago station that was open to the public. It was broadcast at 9:30 a.m. so we had to leave really early to get there. Neither of us had a lot of money, so after taking the streetcar as far south as we could get, we started to hitchhike the rest of the way.

Walking along the side of Highway 41, waving our thumbs, cars kept passing us with nobody stopping to pick us up. We kept on walking south. Eventually we realized that even if we got a lift, it was already too late for Gracie's performance.

We were finally able to get a ride with an old timer who was going to Racine. He agreed to take us to the Northwestern Railroad depot there. For 68 cents apiece, we got one way tickets to Milwaukee, and we didn't have to wait long for the 400, the railroads crack passenger train running between Chicago and Minneapolis to arrive.

Once on board we walked through the train looking for an empty seat. It turned out that we walked from Racine to Milwaukee in half an hour.

Harold and I shared the same bed until I got in the army. When I was 8 or 9, we'd pretend we were squirrels in a nest on a tree and we'd cuddle and talk. Finally, Pa'd stick his head in the door and say, "Ok guys, the first one asleep, whistle." Before we could figure out how to do that, we were asleep.

Miss Purtell, my speech teacher, picked me to represent our high school at a poetry reading thing at the new Pulaski High School on the south side at 26th and Oklahoma. On the Saturday afternoon of the reading, dressed up, and ready to go; I go over there. Each participant was given a poem and a few minutes to read it before going to the mike on stage. My poem was titled "Afeard o' Gals." While reading it with a lot of emphasis where it mattered, I knew my picture was taken.

After I finished, the photographer asked me my name after identifying himself as from the Milwaukee Journal. I had a date that night, but didn't have the car, and after seeing her home around midnight, I went downtown and stood on the 4th Street side of the Journal building watching the presses roll.

I was up before anyone else that Sunday morning, and found my picture in the paper before going back to bed. It wasn't until after lunch before someone else found the picture.

It was in speech class that I met Neil Shultis. At first, we resented each other for whatever reason - maybe because we had some similar problems - Neil was even skinnier than me, weaker, and definitely no athlete.

As we exchanged less than polite epithets at each other, we came to realize both of us were pretty much on the same mental level, gradually comparing notes on our interests.

We were both well-read and keenly interested in, and enjoyed classical music. He also played a good game of chess. His biggest problem was a

Art's Odyssey Unplanned

hyperactive thyroid causing his thin build, and he had some vision problems worse than mine, but he had a great sense of humor. He needed it. One day we were walking west on the south side of Villard Avenue after having a coke at Shorty's restaurant. I suddenly grabbed his arm and walked us across the street in the middle of the block. "Why did we do that", he asked. "Gee Neil, I didn't want old Augie to pull you in" when we walked past the funeral home run by August Abe at the next corner.

Not long after Pa got our first new car, a '36 Chev 4 door, we drove up to a combination picnic and camp grounds on Round Lake, about 65 miles north of us.

I loved the place. It had a decent beach, an old wood building where we changed into our swimming suits or vice versa, and an outdoor privy that didn't smell bad. The lake water was considerably warmer than Lake Michigan.

I especially liked swimming underwater, listening to the sounds of outboard motors way up on the other end of the lake. Ma's Uncle Ollie and Aunt Clara were often there too, with their daughter Lorraine and some of her girlfriends a few years older than me.

As time went on, we discovered some fringe benefits in the old wooden changing house. There were two spaces for the guys, and 2 more for the girls, with some holes in the boy's house closest to the girls. Most of us guys chose the one closest to the girls, and they did the same.

With our backs against the wall away from the one close to the girls, we'd get out of our clothes or swimming suits for a time. Then we'd eyeball the holes in the wall to see the girls who'd done the same, and we all lived happily in the knowledge we now had of the opposite gender.

Entering my sophomore year, I signed up to work on the school paper, *The Custer Chronicle*. Doing whatever had to be done at the moment, I enjoyed the variety of issues that arose, the arguments we had with each other about this, that, or the other thing, each of us passionate about what we thought was the right solution to the problems that came up. I didn't even mind not seeing my name on anything printed in the paper.

Going into my junior year, I decided to enter the tryouts for cheerleader. I figured I'd seen so much of it during football and basketball seasons the last two years it shouldn't be a problem.

We did the tryouts on the auditorium stage in front of the entire student body who were then to vote on who our cheerleaders would be for the coming year.

I went through what I thought were all the right moves and exhortations that would be used at pep rallies, but knew as I performed that something was missing.

We waited in the auditorium while the rest of the student body went to their rooms to vote. That took a while before we were told to report to our classes. There I heard that the principal, scared stiff because of the friends he knew I had, specifically told the rest of the students not to vote for me. I'd enjoyed the try out, and really wasn't bothered by not being chosen.

There was a business course that could be taken as a major that included typing and shorthand for those who intended to be doing office work after graduation. One had to be a Junior to take typing, but an exception was made in my case for two reasons. One was so teachers could read my homework, and the other was that I might do more homework if I could type it. Nobody asked me if we had a typewriter at home. We didn't at the time.

For me, there was another plus factor. I was the only boy in my typing class.

Miss Barron was our teacher, and about the first thing she said was, "The first thing a good typist learns is to blame it on the machine."

When we were 12, there was only eight months' difference between Bobby and I; my birthday in October, and his the following June. His mother arranged for us to take free dancing lessons at a downtown studio on Jefferson Street run by a friend of hers. Neither of us were especially interested, but we got to go downtown on the streetcar in the middle of the week.

For the better part of the year we made the weekly trip, usually stopping somewhere on the way home for an ice cream soda or sundae. We always made for the back of the streetcar where we'd take turns sitting in the motor man's seat.

Sometimes it was already occupied by another kid, so we'd sit on a seat close to the rear door. I'd often bring a Big Little book along to read. One of my favorites was a Big Little book version of a Laurel and Hardy movie. I had no problem laughing out loud as I read, when Bobby'd move to a seat as far from me as he could.

Leona Ludwig was my first girlfriend. Not the prettiest girl in 5th grade, but we got along really well. She had a great sense of humor and we laughed a lot together. After school we'd often walk over to her Dad's saloon on Hopkins Street where we'd sit at the bar and kid around while drinking our sodas. That ended one day when she didn't show up for school. After school, I walked over to the saloon that now had a sign in the door, CLOSED. I never found out why or what happened, but there was nothing I could do about it.

After starting instructions at Atonement, I made friends with some of the kids who went to the church's day school. The more I learned, the happier I was that I went to a public school where the kinds of punishment used by their principle wasn't allowed.

Harold and I often sat in the balcony at the rear of the church. That was also where the organ was placed. The organist was also the principle of the day school.

Harold and I often did the pumping required for the organ to be heard. But, when we knew that one of my friends in his class had been, in our minds, too severely punished, we'd let the organ die at important moments, starting to pump again when we saw the organist getting too hot under the collar, although we knew there wasn't much he could do to us.

Tante Margaret ran a Linen Importing Business out of the Mathews Building. Because of her business, she developed connections with a variety of sources. She got free tickets to the movie *Cleopatra*, starring Claudet Colbert at the Wisconsin Theater downtown.

She, Ma, Bobby, and us three kids took in a matinee. We were totally entranced by the action of the show. Ma was more than a little miffed, especially about us kids seeing Cleopatra's bare breast when committing suicide by letting an Asp bite her bare breast.

If Ma saw a scary movie or heard a frightening radio program, she'd have nightmares for nights after. There was an evening radio show, *Lights Out*, that she wouldn't let us hear. But my friend Kenny Isaacson's folks had no problem with it, so I'd go over there to hear it.

The same thing about going to a movie. If I wanted to see a movie like *King Kong*, Ma'd say "NO." When she'd ask, "What's playing?" I'd tell her the title of the other feature and head for the Ritz on Villard Avenue to see stuff like *King Kong* or *Frankenstein*.

One of my goals was to see a movie in every theater in Milwaukee. Often on weekends, I'd take in a show in one theater on Saturday, and another one on Sunday - usually in the afternoon.

We had the Ritz in north Milwaukee. Tante Margaret, Grandma Schmitz, and Bobby lived on 8th St., and Grandma Hill at 7th and Maple on the south side. I got to the Garfield on 3rd Street, and the Juneau on 6th and Mitchell St., and the Grand on Holton St.

Bobby and I often walked to the Garfield together. Grandma Hill would often send me to Mitchell St. on an errand. I usually made it a point to see what was playing at the Juneau. I knew better than to ask her for the money to take in a movie. I'd tell her what I saw of the still pictures advertising the movie, maybe with a little embellishment. She'd give me the dime to see the film so I could come back and tell her all about it.

On a Sunday afternoon, while the folks were

visiting at Grandma Schmitz's, I took a Center St. streetcar to Holton Street, and a short walk to the Grand. After the movie, realizing I didn't have the carfare to ride back, I walked all the way back to Grandma's place.

They rented an upper flat on the east side of 8th Street between Center Street on the south, and Hadley on the north. It was only two blocks from Borchert Field, the home of the Milwaukee Brewers baseball team.

At 12, we could get into the wooden stadium for free by agreeing to sell Milwaukee Sentinel newspapers in the stands. Bobby and I often did that. It didn't take long for us to learn that we could sell a few papers, and sit back and enjoy the game.

I was 9, and Harold almost 8, when Pa woke us up early one Sunday morning. We had no idea of what was up until after a short breakfast, he went downstairs and came up with stuff we'd never seen before. Three long cane poles with line wrapped around them. Then he took a small carton out of the ice box in the hall.

"I guess we're ready," he said, and steered us out the back door. Once outside, we walked to the bus stop on Stark and Hopkins. Except for handing the carton to me to carry, we got on a south bound #59 bus, getting off to transfer to an east bound bus on Capitol Drive. We got off at Humboldt, and crossing Capitol, we walked along the west bank of the Milwaukee River for a while.

Finally stopping, Pa took the carton from me, and put it on the ground. Then, taking a couple of corks out of his pocket, he fastened them to the now unwound line. From another pocket, he took a small package of hooks, fastening one on the end of each line. Opening the carton, he pulled out a long worm. Breaking it into sections, he put a section of worm on each hook. Casting one out, he gave that pole to Harold, telling him, "If the cork sinks, pull the pole back because that means a fish has bitten the worm. Then he gave the next one to me, with the same order. Finally, he put his in the water.

There wasn't much of a current, so the corks stayed pretty close to where we'd put them. Mine had only been in a few minutes when my cork suddenly disappeared and the line began moving away. I pulled back and felt a strong pull away, but without even thinking about it, I jerked my pole back and ducked as a large fish came flying out of the water, barely missing my head before landing on the ground behind me.

Turning around, I watched my fish, shining in the light, flipping itself this way and that. It was a beauty with shining silvery sides, and red fins and tail. Pa said, "That's a nice Redhorse you've caught." Not really knowing what to do, I asked Pa. "Hold your fish with one hand and try to get the hook out of its mouth with the other. Luckily it wasn't hooked that badly, so I had no problem getting the hook out. It wasn't only the fish that got hooked. I was hooked on fishing

Using some extra twine he had along, Pa tied it to the fish through the gills and the mouth and put it back in the water with one end fastened to a bush on the shore. It wasn't long before Harold landed a Bullhead, then Pa got one, and all of us got some more

Bullheads before we quit. Pa had brought a couple of large paper sacks along, so we had no problem taking our catch home with us on the buses.

I was 10 years old when Prohibition was repealed in 1933. The first Sunday after that, I was designated as the escort to go with Grandma Baker to a Beer Garden at the Plankinton Arcade downtown. Nothing was said to me, but there was no way Pa was going to be able to go with her.

Getting there was no problem; taking the #59 bus on Hopkins St. to the depot at 27th and Keefe, then transferring to the #12 streetcar that took us directly to Plankinton was a cinch.

Pa'd often take Harold and I to the place where we'd watch guys bowling and fish in a fountain there. Now, with artificial palm trees, music, tables and chairs, it made for a pleasant evening. Grandma, usually pretty tight with money, was really enjoying the evening. She'd order a stein of beer, sipping rather than drinking it in gulps, giving me a taste from each stein she had. We stayed there for quite some time, and her glass was never empty.

We finally left, and it didn't take much to see that Grandma was beginning to have problems walking, climbing the steps to board the streetcar and getting down again at the depot. I had a really hard time waking her up on the bus before we had to get off for the short walk home. Only it turned out to be a long walk in terms of the time it took to get home after we got off the bus. Bedtime for us kids was 9 p.m., but it was long after that before we got home, which I didn't mind at all. When my head hit the pillow, I was out immediately.

Art's Odyssey Unplanned

After my 12th birthday, not only could I use streetcars and buses on my own on weekends, but Ma suddenly had an errand boy. She'd buy several of the same women's clothing item, wait until she got home to see which one she really wanted, and then send me to either the Schuster's 12th St. store, Boston Store, or Gimbels downtown to get a credit for those she was returning.

That always gave me an opportunity to go to some of the other places I wanted to go after I took care of Ma's stuff. I'd listen to classical music records at Bradford's record store, hit Woolworth's dime store soda fountain, or one of the shops I patronized for my stamp collection.

I overheard some of our relatives telling Ma how wrong she was to have her son involved with women's underclothing. I laughed to myself when I heard that. Between seeing Ma's and Sis's panties, etc. in the wash and hanging them on the wash line, that was nothing new to me.

It didn't happen often enough to suit me. About once a year, instead of going to school, I'd walk over to 35th Street and Fairmount Ave., meeting there with a bunch of other kids in my grade school class. We'd board a #27 streetcar. I loved the non-stop ride, switching to the #12 tracks at the Hopkins and Keefe Ave. station for the rest of the ride downtown. There our teacher would herd us into the Public Museum for the rest of the morning.

I had an advantage. Ma and Pa, taking advantage of free admission, often took us to the Museum on a Sunday afternoon. Quiet observation was the unwritten rule as we looked at the exhibits. Harold didn't understand that. At one exhibit of Indians going after buffalo, Harold threw a tantrum because we were walking away before the Indian shot the arrow he'd been aiming at a buffalo. Pa had to forcibly carry him away. Once wasn't enough for Harold. At another war exhibit, Harold threw another fit because we were walking away before the soldier pulled the cord that would fire the cannon in front of him.

Although we'd take the return trip a little later than our usual lunch break, we still had time to be home for lunch before going back to school. There wasn't much attention to the rest of the school day, most of our thoughts were involved with what we'd seen at the museum.

Harold and I were offended, because at the Solomon Juneau original trading post at what became Milwaukee, there was the figure of a completely naked Indian boy.

Being sick sometimes had its advantages. Our house was grand central station for most of our relatives. It was on Uncle Ollies area as a gas meter reader for the Gas Company, so he was there on a monthly basis. Ma always had time to enjoy a cup or more of coffee with whatever baked goods she'd have made.

When both he and Grandma Hill were there at the same time, there was always an argument. And, us kids weren't supposed to argue. Her first name was Margaret, and he'd call her "Maggie." She'd tear into him with both barrels, and Ma'd just sit there waiting for things to quiet down. His first name was Alfred, but I guess he didn't mind hearing "Ollie."

Ma'd often yell at us, "Stop that arguing!" My

usual answer was, "We're not arguing, we're having a discussion."

A few days after we'd been to Racine, Grandma was there. Ma said, "Ma, we went to Racine and I couldn't find your marriage certificate for Joe Baker." Grandma's matter of fact answer was, "That's because there isn't one. We married ourselves on the beach there in 1902." Ma knew she'd been born in 1900. She'd learned, when she was 17 that Joe Baker wasn't her real father, but hadn't known till then what the situation really was.

I was 13 when Ma's sister Tante Minnie and her husband moved out to a farm near Mukwonago. Getting tired of listening to the older people talking in the kitchen, I went outside. I saw this horse eating grass.

I managed to get up on its back, figuring I'd get a ride on horseback. Boy, did I! The grey beast had never been ridden before and didn't like the idea, so tore hell-bent for the safety of the barn. Hanging on to its mane for dear life, I saw that the barn door's opening wasn't much higher than the horses back. I scrounged down as close to the horses back as I could, and barely made it through the door. Once in the confines of the barn with nowhere else to go, the horse stopped, and I slid off. Man, talk about thrills!

I barely got out the door when all the grownups came running out of the house, scared stiff that I'd been hurt or killed. They couldn't believe that not only was I okay, but I'd actually gotten a kick out of my wild ride.

Every year I looked forward to Teacher's Convention. This meant that usually in the first week of November, we'd get the Friday off for a long weekend. In my last year of high school, Neil and I decided we'd go to Chicago for a couple of days, using my Y membership for a discounted room at the Y on Wabash. We'd then go out to the Brookfield Zoo to see some exotic animals our Milwaukee Zoo didn't have.

Neil phoned me to tell me that his mother said, "Absolutely not." I went to his house, and his mother told me I couldn't let Neil go to Chicago because, "who knows what kind of things you guys could get into down there." I told her, "Mrs. Shultis, we wouldn't have to go to Chicago to get into stuff like that."

When Ma got home from her job at the laundry that Thursday, she came into our bedroom, sat down on the bed, and started trying to talk me out of going to Chicago. Beating around the bush with generalities, she talked for almost two hours. I just stood there and listened without saying anything.

I slept in on Friday, catching an afternoon train to Chicago and checking in at the Y. Up fairly early, for me, I headed out to the zoo in Brookfield. I couldn't believe how long it took me to get there, using a variety of L trains, and a suburban rail before finally getting there in the early afternoon. But, when I did get there, I decided the trip was worth the effort. Brookfield made our Milwaukee Zoo look like a pet shop by comparison.

Late that afternoon I called Rita Gehl, Jack's younger sister. I was invited to spend the rest of the weekend at their place. So after stopping at the Y to pick up my things and check out, I took the Northwestern Line, getting off at Ravenswood and walking there in time for supper. Rita and I went bowling at an Alley over on Milwaukee and Irving Park, afterwards stopping for a sundae nearby.

Getting back to the house we found a guy from Rita's school waiting for her to get home. I was introduced and things went downhill for me. The guy was a good-looking kid and a real wit with words that had me both jealous and mad at him.

I went to Mass with them Sunday morning, catching a 400 back to Milwaukee that afternoon. Although the Milwaukee Road's Hiawatha trains made the run in the same 75 minutes with fewer stops, I liked the Northwestern better because its trains went faster between stops. There were a few occasions when I'd take the slower North Shore because I liked riding the L tracks between Evanston and the Loop.

It seemed that every February after I started high school, I'd wind up sick at home for a couple of weeks with Bronchitis. I didn't mind that much, although too weak to do much but rest in bed, I was fairly comfortable.

The only fly in the ointment was having Ma rub my chest with stuff like Musterole or Penetro that was supposed to loosen things up in my lungs.

There was a young couple, Ray and Catherine Thomas, that rented the front bedroom. They were a really nice couple. He was a sales rep for a Chicago company; both of them had come from Chicago. Catherine didn't have a job.

He often came home for lunch at the same time I did, and paid me to wipe any bird dung off his car. Catherine was also a stamp collector.

During one of my February sick times, I heard

her and Ma talking over I don't know how many cups of coffee in the kitchen. I was happy to be where they couldn't see me in my dying of embarrassment. Of course, I knew there were differences in what boys had between their legs, but I'd never imagined that this was something women talked about among themselves! And the most embarrassing part was hearing Ma talk about Harold's and my circumcisions after we were born! If I could have crawled any lower into the mattress I would have. I couldn't even bring myself to talk to Ma about how I felt afterwards.

For Christmas when I was 13, I got a pair of hockey ice skates. There were plenty of places around town where we could skate with no charge. There was a fairly large empty lot on the west side of Hopkins St. that the city flooded and then let freeze. A small warming shed went up next to it, and we could change into our skates inside before going out on the ice.

Late one winter afternoon, Pa and Ma came over to Hopkins St. to watch me skate. For the first time in my life, I felt extraordinarily graceful as I glided across the frozen field. When I got home, Ma asked me why I seemed to be so stiff on the ice. All I could say in my sense of disappointed devastation was that I didn't feel that way.

The lagoon at Silver Spring park froze over as well, and there was a larger shed on the shore. It was worth the walk up there for the much larger skating area. But, it closed much too early for us in the evening at 9 o'clock. We'd get our stuff out of the shed, and stay on the ground for a while after the lights went out.

Art's Odyssey Unplanned

Then we'd be back on the ice, playing games like crack the whip, that we couldn't do when the officials were there. The game meant skating in kind of a circle at high speed, and suddenly stopping. Playing crack the whip one evening with our friend Bob Gropp at the front end of a group of us, and Harold at the other, we cracked the whip so to speak, and Harold went flying, winding up face down on the snow of the bank.

We stopped the game, picked him up for the fairly long walk home, and brought him in the house with a pretty bloody face and a lot on his clothes. He was too macho to let himself cry, but it must have hurt pretty bad. Whether she knew something had to be done or what, but Ma for once didn't faint at the sight of her bloody son, took him in the bathroom and got him cleaned up pretty good. Luckily Harold hadn't been hurt very badly, because a few nights later we were playing crack the whip again.

Part 3.

Unless one of us was pumping the organ, Harold and I usually sat in the front seats of the balcony at church. Old Pastor Schaefer stopped in the middle of a sentence in his sermon, and pointing his hand upwards; called us by name, ordering us to immediately stop doing it.

We stopped dropping pop bottle caps down from over the rail. Nothing more was said until we got home and Sis cried about how embarrassing it was for her.

Pastor had a habit of emphasizing his points by waving his hand in the air with just the index finger and little finger showing, the two middle fingers held by his thumb. He was totally unaware that for us, this was the symbol we used to tell other kids that something they said was bull shit to us. And some sitting around us wondered why we giggled on such occasions.

We probably should have felt sorry for Ma. She did a lot of babysitting when she was a kid, taking on kids nobody else would. As she described it, most of the babies she took care of were Down Syndrome or Hydrocephalic kids who were pretty helpless and docile. She looked forward to having kids of her own, but was totally unprepared for three fairly intelligent, selfishly driven, and usually in conflict with their siblings, kids.

She looked forward to having kids who would play dolls or house with her at home, but even Sis as she grew did things away from the house with her girlfriends.

We always had cats, it seemed, and each of us had our own kitten after Grandma Baker's cat Mitzi came home after being out in the cold for several nights with her ears partly frozen off. My little white kitten was Mopsy. In summer, I'd catch grasshoppers and feed them to her, but there was a time when she was too eager for her treat and bit my finger instead. The finger healed well, but there were no more grasshoppers for Mopsy. Later, when I'd be soaking my foot in a hot chamomile tea concoction for an ingrown toenail problem, I'd take Mopsy on my lap and pet her until she purred up a storm.

With no income of her own, but a fierce sense of independence, Grandma Baker would have me pull our coaster wagon on her weekly trek to the County Relief Station on Hopkins Street. There, with a lot of other people needing help to have something to eat, we'd wait our turn to get stuff like bags of flour, sugar, and other food stuff to take home in the wagon. I kind of liked doing it, and not just because it was another place to go.

I don't know if it was because I had the longest legs of us kids, or the loudest voice, but I was always the one Pa picked to get Harold and Sis to come home for supper. Of course, Pa knew I'd have a better idea of where they were than he did.

When I was 9, Pa wound up in a hospital in

Waukesha. We didn't have a car, but Hans - Ruth Seerup's boyfriend - took Ma and I to Waukesha one evening. I'd never been in any other car that took me that far. We spent a couple of hours visiting Pa, and he wasn't confined to a bed. He didn't seem sick to me. Although we had a nice visit, I couldn't wait till I could have the thrill of another fast ride back home. I never bothered to wonder why I was taken along, and the other kids left at home with Grandma Baker's supervision.

My cousin Dorothy, several years older than I was, often stayed at our place. I got really mad at her when I was 8, and swung a string of large wooden beads against her, hitting her in the back so hard she cried.

She must have forgiven me over the years, because later she'd take me with her to the Neue Apostoliche Kierche, The New Apostolic Church, on 4th St. and Wright when Ma couldn't. And, when I was a teenager, and Dorothy had a job, she'd take me to movies downtown with her, and have some treat afterwards. One of them starred Bobby Breen, who was younger than I was, so I guess wasn't old enough to be embarrassed when his swim trunks came off showing his bare butt in the water.

Well or sick, I didn't miss watching a football or basketball game in my four years at Custer. I wasn't up on the technical details of either sport, but I loved the pep element of the cheerleaders and watching the band in their striking uniforms of white pants and bright red tunics as they performed their maneuvers and music at half-time on the field. Sis switched from violin to clarinet when learning that violins weren't

Art's Odyssey Unplanned

included in the instrumental makeup of the band.

I enjoyed watching and listening to the band, but wasn't interested in playing in it. I did want to play something though. Sis's clarinet looked too complicated for me, so I thought I'd try to play trumpet.

We rented a trumpet from Beihoff's at 51st and North Ave., and I signed up for the same kind of lessons as I'd had for the violin. Only this time, the lessons were given at Roosevelt Junior High School on Walnut St. The instructions were worse than for the violin. The teacher told the group of us to play middle C. Again, I didn't know how to ask what I had to do to play middle C.

Somewhere along the line, we paraphrased the Notre Dame pep song to our own version. *Beer, Beer for old Custer High, bring on the whiskey, bring on the Rye. Send a freshman out for gin, don't let a sober person in. We never stagger, we never fall, we sober up on wood alcohol, while the faculty comes staggering, back from the brewery.*

While it was fairly softly suggested, it was clear that we were not to indulge in such a parody in public. The warning was not so softly completely ignored.

Neither Harold or I were much good at memorizing prose material, so when it came time to prepare our material for the Christmas program at church, we were up a tree. Fortunately, we were part of a group that had to recite Bible passages having to do with the birth of Jesus. Nobody else knew that Harold and I, standing up with the rest of our group, didn't know our parts, as the other kids in the group did the recitation. Sis, being in a different group had no problem reciting her passages, but let everyone at home know how disgraced she felt about her brother's dereliction of their Christmas duty.

A couple of weeks before Christmas, the alcove between the parlor and the dining room was closed off by a white sheet hung from one side of the room to the other. Even the relatives had to use the rear door to come in or go out. Even the sides of the sheet were fastened to the walls.

Finally, on Christmas eve, after coming home from church, we hung about in the dining room, hearing strange noises and deep grunts from the parlor side of the sheet. After a while we heard a deep bass "Ho, Ho, Ho" and then silence.

A few minutes later, Pa came in the rear door in his mailman's uniform, taking his hat off, and saying he'd seen a strange figure going out the front door. We'd better check this out, he said, taking down the sheet revealing a well-lighted great Christmas tree with all kinds of Christmas presents laid out on a white cloth at its base.

Holding hands, everyone who was there that evening, stood and sang "Silent Night." Then us kids sat down and waited for Pa to hand out the presents, a lot of them going to the grownups before we got any. From some of the grownups we got clothing items they thought we needed, but there were also the kinds of toys that Ma and Pa knew we'd like.

After all the gifts were opened, and us kids given a chance to try out our toys, we went to the kitchen for a Christmas feed. That was only the beginning. For once we were allowed to play with our new toys till we got so tired we couldn't anymore, and that didn't happen till well into the morning of Christmas Day.

Of course, there was some chagrin because Harold and I warmed up to the 25 cent toy soldiers Pa gave us, in preference to the more expensive clothing items from some of the relatives, like new underwear or handkerchiefs.

It wasn't a Christmas thing, but one year Grandma Baker made new pajamas for Harold and me. We'd been subjected to being measured for them without knowing why we were being measured. When they were finished, we were asked to try them on. Harold and I looked at each other and refused to even touch them. They were the most gosh awful looking tops and bottoms we'd ever seen.

Ma said something to the effect that we should appreciate all the time and work Grandma took to make them, but that didn't cut any ice with us. We found ourselves between a rock and a hard place when we went to get ready for bed.

The new pajamas were on a chair in our room, but we couldn't find the one's we'd been wearing. Both of us got undressed, but got into bed wearing our underwear that night. The next night we were told to put our underwear outside our door and Ma'd put them in the wash. Doing that, we went to our drawer for a different set of underwear only to find the drawer was empty. We did something we'd never done before. We slept naked that night.

The next evening, Ma, usually fairly mild about making us do things, was adamant.

"Tonight, whether you guys like it or not, you're

wearing those new pajamas if I have to stay here and watch you put them on. I'm going to step out in the hall, and when I come in again, you're gonna be wearing those pajamas." We were past the point where we wanted to be naked in front of grownups like that, so we cringed and put them on.

Ma came in to make sure we'd put them on. "Now guys" she said, "Make sure you keep them on because me and Pa are going to be checking. What she didn't know was the miracle that had taken place. The new pajamas, ugly as they were, were made of an incredibly soft flannel and the most comfortable things I'd ever worn. I loved them, and so did Harold.

Not too long after that, just as Harold and I got out of our pajamas to get dressed for the day, Grandma Baker walked in on us. "Grandma," we yelled, "get out of here, we're naked." "So," she said, "I've seen a lot more than you guys got!" Leaving us in shocked bewilderment as we realized what she meant.

Tante Margaret worked for a company that had its annual picnic at Gonrings resort on Big Cedar Lake every year. A friend of hers took our families out there in his car. There were a lot of games we could play, food, ice cream cones or bars, sodas for us kids, and beer for the grownups. And there was music. There was an old man walking around playing a violin. I followed him, listening to all the beautiful music he was giving us.

Being on a fairly large lake, there were row boats to use. Pa was more than willing to take us out for rides, but Grandma Schmitz and Bobby's mother wouldn't let him go with us. They said, "The boat might tip over, and all of you could drown." They had the same attitude toward swimming, they'd never let Bobby learn to swim.

Once we were away from the shore, Pa moved to the seat in front of him, telling me to take his seat, and he'd teach me how to row a boat. It was so easy for me that he let me do most of the rowing that afternoon.

There was one time at Bobby's house when all of us kids were talking about doing something that we weren't sure we'd be allowed to do. Bobby's comment was, "Just do what I do, throw a tantrum and keep it up till they give in." Harold, Sis and I just looked at him. We knew that wouldn't work for us.

We knew we had it a lot better than he did. He was scared of his own shadow. He was afraid of the dark and needed a light on when he went to bed. Grandma and the Tante scared him with threats of the Boogey Man to get him to do what they wanted.

I often spent the night at their place, both on Keefe Avenue and at 8th St. Bobby didn't seem to have a problem when I was with him. I loved to listen to the chimes of an old antique wind up clock they had.

They were living with us when Ma had her tonsillectomy. After seeing her in a bloody mess at the hospital, I had a hard time getting to sleep. It was well after midnight when I had to use the bathroom. The door to the front bedroom where Tante Margaret, Grandma Schmitz, and Bobby slept was open, and I heard Tante Margaret talking to Grandma.

Leaving the bathroom door partly open, I listened horrified at what I heard. Tante Margaret was sure Ma would die. Then she'd take over running this house and do things the way she thought they should be done! Everything she said sounded worse to me than what she'd just finished saying. It sounded as if Pa wouldn't have any say about anything.

I couldn't wait for Pa to get home the next day. As soon as I could, I told him every detail of what I'd heard during the night. After supper Pa went to see Ma. When he got home he told us she was doing better, but it'd be a few days before she could come home.

Then he asked everyone to sit in the parlor. In very definite language he told his sister, Grandma could stay if she wanted to, but she and Bobby would have to leave in a week's time. He didn't say a word about why. He just told them things weren't working out for us, and they'd have to go. In less than a week, Tante Margaret, Bobby, and Grandma Schmitz moved to an upper flat on 8th Street.

It was while they were still living with us that our family and Grandma Schmitz were going somewhere on a rainy September evening. I hadn't wanted to go, but Pa made me get in the car. Sitting in the back seat with Grandma, I was crying the blues about being there. Grandma turned to me and said, "Boyce, laugh and the world laughs with you, cry, and you cry alone." I stopped crying.

After they moved, Bobby went to the 5th Street school. That school seemed to have a lot of evening activities going on. Tante Margaret and Grandma never went. Instead they'd call us, and Pa would take us and Bobby to whatever was going on. I got to hear some great music from orchestras that donated their time to play there. I soon realized that when they'd play a symphony piece, it was always only the final movement; that was where the most melody and action seemed to be.

Although I'd ridden on other kids' two wheel bikes, I'd never rode one on my own, so the first time I got on my own bike, I had some balancing problems that I found I could solve by going fast. Barreling down the middle of our short street as fast as I could go, I wasn't ready for what happened.

A small girl on the west side of the street saw her Dad on the other side and started to run across the street, but wound up falling to the pavement after running into the front wheel of my bike, stopping me in the middle of the street.

Scared stiff, I was speechless when her Dad walked over, picked up his daughter, and without saying a word to me, scolded his daughter for running out without looking where she was going. Luckily there was no damage to my new bike, but I realized I was going to have to learn how to ride slower and still keep my balance. It wasn't long before I was doing just that.

Ma was a real worry wart, but she would have been worried sick if she saw the places I rode my bike, and the things my friends and I did with our bikes, some right across the street from our house.

There was an empty field between 38th Street and Hopkins Street, but its surface was about a foot and a half above the sidewalk. A group of us would start out on one side or the other, ride across as fast as we could go, and jump our bikes over the edge, trying to hit the street below without landing on the sidewalk or the grass between the sidewalk and the street.

On one occasion, although succeeding, I wound

up with a fairly good sized hole in the tire wall. No problem. Although the inner tube gradually formed a small balloon sticking out the side of the tire, I waited till it blew out before getting a new tube and tire.

There was a kind of inter-family rivalry among the grownups on the Schmitz side of the relation. Within days of getting my bike, Grandma Schmitz bought a bike for Bobby. It was quite a bit fancier than my bike.

Not long after that, he and I decided to head up to Doctor's Park on the lake, some distance north of town. He wasn't used to riding his bike in the heavy traffic we encountered on our way north.

We hadn't planned on doing any swimming, and when we got to the beach there was nobody else around, so we started skipping stones across the water. Luckily, we hadn't thrown too many when some kind of park official came over, chewed us out, and in a show of his authority, ordered us to retrieve the stones we'd tossed and bring them back to the shore.

We didn't mind that at all. In fact, it gave us an excuse to get in the water, so we spent a lot of time wading around the area, picking up some stones as we felt like it, actually picking up a lot more than we'd thrown.

It took us forever to get back to 8th Street. Bobby was pooped, so after a short ride from the park, we pretty much walked the rest of the way.

Just before the 4th of July when I was 17, Kenny Isaacson, Bobby, and I decided to bike to Oconomowoc - about 32 miles west of Milwaukee. We had a small pup tent with us. Kenny and I left home about 3 o'clock in the morning of the 2nd, Bobby chickening out at the last minute.

Heading south to Capitol Drive, we were stopped by a cop asking us what we were doing at that time of the morning. We told him where we were going, and he asked our names. He asked me, "Your last name's Schmitz, what does your Dad do for a living?" When I told him Pa was a mailman, the cop said "Oh, I know Schmitty, go on guys."

The sun had come up before we got to Oconomowoc, but it was still early so we pitched our little tent in Winnie Harrigan's back yard, crawled in and slept for a while.

Later, cousin Dorothy came out and woke us to say that Ma was on the phone. I wasn't surprised. When they'd woke up and saw that I was gone, Ma called Bobby and found out where we were.

"Get on your bikes, and come home right now!" "Ma" I countered, "It's 4th of July with all the holiday traffic on the road. You wanna get us killed!" I knew that would do it. "Well then, come home after the holiday when you know it's safe." We stayed there the rest of the week.

Winnie Harrigan was a friend of Tante Margaret's and ran a woman's clothing store on the main street of the town, and had hired Dorothy to work for her. We wound up having all our meals with them.

Winnie's brother had a row boat he kept there for an easy launch into Lake Labelle, the main reason we went there. During the warm July days, Kenny and I'd swim and take the boat out for some fishing, sharing our catch, that we'd clean, with the women.

In the evening, we'd take them out for a boat ride, Kenny and I taking turns with the oars. The following weekend we biked back home.

Going east, we had to laugh at a dog racing us on the other side of the road. Watching us, it ran smack into a low metal sign, sitting down in a daze. At one point a pickup with some kids in the back passed us. As they did so, the kids threw empty glass milk bottles at us. A couple of police dogs came after us, but we were prepared for that. We had squirt guns with ammonia instead of water in them. That took care of the dogs.

In late August of 1938, we headed north in our '34 Plymouth towing a small trailer Pa'd borrowed from a friend. With Pa driving, Ma in the other front seat, Grandma and Grandpa Hill and us three kids in the back seat, it was more than cozy.

Ma wanted to see the Dionne quintuplets who were now 4 years old, and Grandma didn't believe there was any such thing, and us kids couldn't have cared less. We weren't in any great hurry, so although we had a cabin for the night on the American side of the locks at Saulte St. Marie, Pa took us to the Canadian side because the busiest boat traffic was on their side.

I was intrigued. During summer school English class, I'd read a story about a kid on the shore communicating with guys on the long ore boats I was now watching traverse the locks of the canal. If I'd been invited to board one of those vessels I'd have jumped at the chance. We spent most of the day there before going back to the American side.

To do so, we had to go through Customs again,

Art's Odyssey Unplanned

and this time had a serious problem. Pa'd told everyone to say they were from Milwaukee. Grandma said she was from Germany, Grandpa said he was from England. Ma and Pa said Milwaukee, and us kids weren't asked. The official okay'd all of us except Pa. They wouldn't let him return to the state side because of his strong German accent. Things were getting dicey in Europe, and Canada was a British dominion. Pa hadn't learned English till he was 7 years old, and then didn't need it much in the Milwaukee of his childhood. Pa was the only one who could drive. Us kids didn't mind staying on the Canadian side. Pa finally realized he had his U.S. Army discharge papers from World War I with him. After showing them, he was allowed to drive us back to our American cabin.

The next day we drove into Canada, but didn't stop at the locks again. Driving east, we spent a night at Algoma Mills. I would have been happy to stay right there, and the heck with the quintuplets. There was a good-sized lake there, and we saw a guy with absolutely the biggest fish I'd ever seen outside of the Chicago Aquarium. It was a beauty of a Lake Trout that he'd caught using a wire line. I could see that any lesser line couldn't have landed that fish. Soon after, we were on our way again.

Grandma hated going anywhere beyond places she could go on foot, or streetcar and bus, and constantly let us know about it. Grandpa was always a pretty quiet guy.

We finally got to North Bay, a town just a short distance from Callander where the quintuplets were to be seen playing outside when weather permitted. But, there was an almost steady drizzle, so we holed up waiting for the weather to clear.

Spending some time at the post office to mail cards, I made a discovery. Natives of the place tossed envelopes of mail received into waste buckets. I'd tip them to an angle where I could reach in and get envelopes with sometimes high denominations of Canadian stamps for my collection.

I knew when I got home I'd have to soak them off, but I was used to doing that anyway. There were times when Ma wanted a bowl, she'd look in our room to see if it was being used to soak stamps.

During the rainy days, Pa'd take us out to the shore of the lake and Harold and I'd try to outdo each other with skipping stones on the water. Finally, the sun came out.

We drove over to Callander, and I have to admit, it was kind of fun to see these 5 little girls playing outside, apparently completely oblivious to the crowd watching them.

In a building next to their play area, was a souvenir shop, featuring Mr. Dionne giving autographs for a dollar each. Not at all interested in his signature, I spent some of the money I'd saved on a small set of the Royal Canadian Mounted Police on horseback.

Ma was thrilled to have seen the quintuplets. Grandma laughed at her for being fooled into believing that those five kids were all sisters. Now, mission accomplished, we headed easterly for home.

We had to stop at Welland, whether we wanted to or not. The car developed a problem that had to be fixed if we were to get home. I didn't mind. It gave me a lot of time to watch the bridge and the shipping traversing the Welland Canal.

While waiting, we went to a tavern where Grandpa could enjoy the Ginger Beer he couldn't get at home. Us kids had sodas. Ma and Grandma committed a serious faux pas when they sat at the bar with Pa and Grandpa. In Canada, the women sat at a place away from the bar.

Eventually, with the car fixed, we rode past Lake Ontario, Toronto, and Hamilton to the Canadian side of Niagara Falls.

Us kids wanted to go for a ride on the *Maid of the Mist* cruising the river below the falls, but boats were anathema to Grandma, so that was out. The sidewalk along the side of the river and the falls featured a heavy mist from the falls. As we walked along, Grandma complained, as usual, "We'll drown before we finish here."

There was a great sidelight to the quintuplet's story. Doctor Dafoe was at the birth, and became something of a hero, to the point where stories and movies were made about his work as the fictitious name, Dr. Christian, was used in the media. I think I saw all the movies and read all the stories about the guy.

Getting to Windsor, Ontario, with Grandma's feeling about boats, my preference for taking the ferry to Detroit was out of the question, so Pa drove us across Ambassador Bridge instead of using the tunnel where we wouldn't see anything. Once home, I was eager to show my bounties to my friends, and do the needed soaking of the stamps I'd found.

In 2nd grade, I saw another kid take something

out of the teacher's open purse on her desk. A few days later I felt devastated for having told her. The next day the guy wasn't in class, but it wasn't till later that we found out why. That morning he was killed by a car while crossing Hopkins St. on his way to school. I couldn't shake the feeling that if I hadn't told the teacher, it wouldn't have happened.

By the time I reached high school I was developing a lot of new interests, most of which required money that I never had enough of. Sure, I got a quarter a week allowance, and the pittance I got for peddling the weekly shopping paper. Yet, I did seem to have enough for when I really wanted something.

After Grandpa Baker died, Grandma occupied the room on the west end of the attic. Always busy doing something, she'd fall asleep on her bed after supper. She'd snore up a storm that could be heard downstairs. One evening when Ma and Pa were busy with something, I cut into an onion that I took upstairs and, without it touching her face, moved it back and forth below Grandma's nose. When I saw her waking up with the snoring stopped, I quietly left the room, and not long after Grandma came downstairs to listen to her favorite radio show; *Amos and Andy*.

The house on the southeast corner of 38th St. and Stark St. was owned by the grandparents of Sis's friend Wanny. The upper flat was rented to a young couple with a small son. They hired Grandma to babysit him.

That didn't last long, Grandma needed more money because Grandpa Baker left absolutely nothing when he died. Soon she was working as a live-in caretaker for an old lady living out on 47th and

Hampton, three blocks west of the city limits.

On New Year's Eve, the couple with the small son asked me to babysit for him. That's when I learned that Eddy Kaupla was 5 years old. I was 12. I got there at 8 that evening. Eddy went to bed at 8:30 and I was stuck for the rest of the time until Mr. and Mrs. Kaupla rolled in at 3 the next morning. I was disappointed to get only a quarter, but took it. Actually, Eddy was a good kid, and we took to each other, becoming really good friends.

For whatever reason, Grandma Baker moved from one such job to another fairly often. My guess is that she was used to doing things her way, whether anybody else liked it or not.

Another such job was taking care of an invalid woman on a farm in Marcy, about 20 miles straight out West Hampton Ave. Again, we were the ones who went to see Grandma.

The farmer and his wife were Hollanders. His English was limited, but hers was pretty good. While Ma and Pa visited with Grandma, his wife let me play their Victrola and I got to hear music I'd never heard before. There were some neat records like "Comin' Through the Rye" and other Scottish songs that I enjoyed being able to sing long after we left the farm.

Not long after Grandma left the Dutch couple, somehow or other she found a job taking care of the arthritic wife of a man on Milwaukee's south side at 7th St. and Maple St. Mrs. Hill was bound to a wheel chair, but was also very pleasant to us when we visited Grandma. There was no time off for Grandma.

Mr. Hill worked for the TMER&L at the Kinnickinnick streetcar Barns at Mitchell Street and

KK as we called it. He didn't drive, and walked to and from work.

Grandma was out of a job again when Mrs. Hill died. She was laid out in the living room. Harold insisted on going in the back door. He didn't want to be in the same room with a dead body. The undertaker was there and told Harold, "it's only live people who can hurt you." It was only a month or so later that Mr. Hill called and asked Grandma to come back as his housekeeper. She was more than happy to do that.

I was just as happy, because Grandma often put me to work doing things like turning the big mangle she had in our basement that she used to smooth stuff that got wrinkled in the wash. It wasn't a hard job, but took me away from other things I wanted to do, like going to a grass fire when I heard the sirens going down Hopkins St.

She was only there about three months, when we had the party at our house, celebrating the wedding of Grandma and Danny Hill.

It wasn't long after that when Harold and I stayed at the Hill house as we had with Grandma in that old tar paper shack. But this time, it didn't take long to know that Harold couldn't stay there.

Feather beds were the thing there, and Harold wound up in total misery, almost stopping breathing. So I wound up staying weekends there by myself.

Maybe it was because Grandma didn't really know how to get to the New Apostolic Church from 7th and Maple, even though she had relatives who went there, she didn't. Because Danny worked for the TMER&L, she could have ridden for free.

Art's Odyssey Unplanned

I didn't mind sleeping in on a Sunday morning, waking up to the sounds of the bells of several churches, mostly catholic, in the area. It got so that I could tell which church by the way the bells sounded.

I liked the popular music and the classical stuff, but I liked a lot of the novelty songs too. There was "Flat Foot Floogie With a Floy Floy." We'd sing that when we'd walk past a cop on his beat. Another went something like this, "Beans, beans, the musical fruit, the more you eat, the more you toot."

One Sunday afternoon, we'd taken the #35 streetcar to the end of the line. From there we walked a short distance to the brand-new viaduct that hadn't been opened to the public yet. On the west side of the viaduct we walked on the sidewalk to the south end.

There was a cop there. He told Pa, "You guys aren't supposed to be walking on the viaduct; it hasn't been opened to the public yet. So, go back to where you came from."

Pa let us know with a look that we weren't to break up laughing at the cops' ridiculous order, so we did as the cop told us and walked back to the north end of the new viaduct.

As good as a lot of things were, it always seemed as if there was a dark side to life. In grade school, there were the taunts and bullying I experienced. Because I wasn't a fighter, I was called a coward, yellow, and a few other things.

That ended when we got into high school, because like all the guys, I'd developed other interests, like seeing girls I liked. One was Martha, the good-looking girl at the locker next to mine. She was as sweet as could be, but when we were out on the one date we had, I realized she wasn't interested in much of anything that I liked.

I was surprised she'd even gone out with me, but I guess she was as desperate as I was. Looking in the mirror at home, I saw an ugly, skinny guy, no muscle, wearing glasses. I thought to myself, that old thing about "Boys don't make passes at girls who wear glasses," works both ways.

There were times, working the checking room at the Saturday evening dances, I was ready to quit, so I could go down to the gym and at least try to get a girl to dance with me, but I knew Ma'd have a fit if I quit a fairly decent paying job, and I usually needed the money.

A fringe benefit of having Leo and Jack Gehl staying with us, was that Froeming Florist on the south side would hire me to work on Saturday's to do odd jobs around the shop. One Saturday Mr. Froeming had me assembling corsage boxes in a side room. It didn't take me that long, so when I finished I sat in a corner reading a comic book I had in my back pocket. Mr. Froeming came in, and before giving me another job to do, told me, "If you're not busy, LOOK busy." I got the message.

There were times when Jack, done for the day, would take Harold and I out for an evening drive with him. While gassing up his car, Jack asked me to check the tires. Some filling stations had air pressure gauges on the hose, but this one didn't. I got knocked on my butt when the tire exploded. That didn't hurt nearly as much as what I was afraid of Jack thinking of me.

Going to the trunk, he took out a wrench, telling me, "We'll jack up the car, you loosen the nuts, and we'll put on the spare." With the three of us working together it didn't take that long to get us back on the road again. That required stopping for an ice cream soda before going home.

My locker partner was a nice guy, Andy Schoen. We became close friends in no time. His home life was the pits. I never knew if his real father had died, or been divorced but his parents had a different surname.

Because they lived some distance north of Silver Spring Road, they had to pay tuition for Andy to go to Custer, and provide transportation for him. Because we had different lunch hours, he'd sometimes let me drive his father's brand new Chev home for lunch.

After the Pearl Harbor event, disgusted with school, and even more disgusted with his home life, he came over to our house after school one day to tell us he was quitting school to join the navy. I told him, "You can try that, but without that diploma, the navy wouldn't even look at you." We graduated together, but almost immediately he joined the navy. I envied him. They wouldn't take me in the navy.

On a weekend after I knew he'd finished his boot camp, I took the North Shore to The Great Lake's Navy Training Center.

I waited, with a lot of other people, just outside the main gate. We saw a large formation of sailors marching toward the gate. Reaching the gate, an officer gave a command, and hordes of blue jackets broke formation and ran out the gate. But, for some reason unknown to me, Andy wasn't among them. I never saw him again.

Bobby's home life hadn't been much better than Andy's, so as soon as he was 18, he dropped out of high school and joined the army. Because Pa'd been in the infantry, that's what he signed up for. I split a gut laughing when I heard that, because if anyone hated walking, it was Bobby.

After graduation, one of my jobs was working in the stock room of a dime store near Forest Home Ave. and Mitchell Street. There I learned that a 10-cent bottle of cheap perfume was a money maker for the store that paid ten dollars for a carton of 1,000 bottles.

Another florist, this time on the east side would occasionally hire me to deliver plants, corsages, and other floral offerings to funeral homes, churches, and hospitals. I already knew, from riding with Jack, that Deaconess Hospital had the slowest elevators in the country, which was a real pain in cold weather when one had a truck loaded with stuff for a lot of other places. This truck had features I'd never heard of and made for some hairy experiences in heavy traffic before I figured things out.

Another job was with a wholesale butcher. It meant getting up fairly early, which was often hard for the night owl me. Getting to his warehouse on the east side wasn't easy.

Except for eating my share of it through the years, I knew nothing about the differences between raw beef, pork or veal, especially in their whole carcasses.

After loading the truck as ordered, I began my deliveries to individual butcher shops, but as the days went on, I developed a guilty conscience about the greenish coating on the carcasses I delivered, and finally, after a couple of weeks quit the job. It wasn't much later that I learned the value of "aged beef." I never thought of asking the boss about it.

Not only was I still sitting for Eddy Kaupla, but he seemed to enjoy going to different places around town with me. He was too trusting, and one day I couldn't resist taking advantage of that. It was a nice warm summer day and the garden hose was out after being used to water the lawn.

I told Eddy, look into this and you'll see a monkey after I handed him the nozzle.

While he strained his eye to see the monkey, I went to the side of the house and turned the water on. He was too surprised to cry, but got a good soaking. Taking him upstairs to get the change of clothing he needed, he told his mother what had happened. Expecting her to read me the riot act, I was stunned when all she did was get Eddy into some dry clothes. I loved that woman!

We had a variety of people renting that front bedroom. There was a young couple, Bill and Ann with a small baby girl, Joy Ann. Ann was a stay-at-home mother, and Bill was a used car salesman who seemed to make enough to enable them to go out often. If I wasn't sitting with Eddy, as often as not, I'd be taking care of Joy Ann and getting better paid for doing so, because she needed more than I'd ever done before - like frequent diaper changes and baths.

Before the folks began renting that bedroom, we had a mother and her two young sons living with us for a while. The parents belonged to the New Apostolic Church and lived a few blocks south of us.

This was during the height of the depression. One morning the Mrs. sent one of the boys upstairs to let his father know that breakfast was ready. The kid screamed and crying, ran down to tell his mother something was wrong up there. She went up and found her husband hanging from a rafter with a small note nearby. He'd been laid off his job at A.O. Smith, one of the big employers in the area.

Without any income to make the mortgage payments, Mrs. B. and the boys moved in with us. A little older than Sis, they were younger than Harold or me.

Harold and I would have beat up on the boys, but Ma and Pa made it clear that we couldn't say or do anything to hurt them. Too young for us to realize the terrible trauma they'd experienced, we endured their constant misbehavior, beating up on us, cursing us out in language we didn't dare use, until they finally moved out. We weren't interested in keeping in touch, although Ma did.

Probably the best folks we had in that bedroom were the Thomas's. Catherine and Ma really hit it off, and Ray's schedule was pretty flexible, so on a nice summer day he'd ask us if we wanted to go swimming. The three of us would get in his car with Catherine and away we'd go, often to a beach on the lake where we wouldn't have to pay. The funny thing was that Ray couldn't swim but enjoyed being in the water with us.

He was full of humor. Catherine didn't like it when he'd sing, "I love to go swimmin, with bowlegged women, and dive between their legs." Harold and I thought it was hilarious.

Art's Odyssey Unplanned

Before I could use the bus pass on my own, we met my oldest cousin Ervin, Ma's nephew, on the back seat of a bus one Sunday afternoon. I couldn't understand why he seemed so happy with four girls who were with him. He got really messed up when, trying to introduce them, he got their names all mixed up. Later, I found out he did that on purpose, but the girls didn't appreciate it.

I didn't understand it, and didn't know how to ask about it, but there were times when we were out with Pa that he seemed to be totally preoccupied as if he was in another world. Spanking, if done at all, was usually just a few light swaps with a wooden spoon, or if it was a case of swearing, a small dose of cream of tartar. When in my late teens, I painted the handle of the wooden spoon in stripes of a variety of colors and put it back in the drawer.

Ma, and Grandma Hill, when she was with us, did a lot of baking, making frequent use of vanilla. I loved the aroma of the stuff, and kept pestering Ma to let me have some. She never would, and I didn't have the nerve to sneak any. One day, out of desperation, Ma gave me a teaspoonful of vanilla, telling me I could have it, but I had to take the full spoonful. I agreed, and she gave it to me – but good! I couldn't understand how something could smell so good, and taste so terribly bad.

The 4th of July was one of my favorite holidays. We'd walk over to school in the morning. There, with friends we hadn't seen since June, we'd get flags to carry, form into groups, and start the walk to Smith Park. On the way, instead of singing patriotic songs, we'd sing "I scream, you scream, we all scream for ice cream." We knew we'd each get a Dixie Cup of ice cream when we got there.

Often, Bobby'd stay with us for the night before, and I'd have the leather davenport in the parlor. I'd lay there awhile, listening to early birds setting off their fireworks.

After lunch, we'd hike back to Smith Park for the coaster and buggy parade. We'd spend weeks, with help from Ma and Grandma Baker, creating patriotic floats for Harold and I, and for Sis with a buggy. We usually got some fairly decent prizes for our efforts.

Ma was really put out one year. Sis won a first prize and had a choice between some kind of metallic covered purse and a pair of roller skates. Sis chose the skates that eventually I wound up using.

In the evening, it was back to Smith Park for the fireworks that were worth the "oohs and ahhs" they elicited. After grade school days, Pa'd sometimes take us to Reservoir Park on the east side. We'd climb the steps to the top of the huge hill that contained a reservoir for the city's water system of years past. From the top we had great views of the fireworks to the east.

Even if I had a job during the summer, it was a daytime job, leaving my evenings free for whatever kind of fun there was to be had. Jack Langtry's folks were divorced, and he lived in an upper flat with his mother. She was one of the young at heart people, and we looked at her as akin to an aunt.

In July of 1941, Jack's uncle, aunt, and cousins from Clearwater, Florida came up for a couple of weeks visit. The oldest girl, Carol was 16, and we liked each other. I took her to a couple of movies.

Everything was fine until Jack's uncle took us to a drive in Frozen Custard stand. We were the third car in line, the car ahead of us being a convertible with the top down. When Jack's uncle saw the black kids in that car, he waited till it was our turn to order.

Instead of ordering, he just drove through, stopping at a store on the way home to pick up a package of ice cream. Along the way, he angrily told us that no way was he going to patronize an establishment that permitted blacks to be served ahead of whites, and in the same place as whites.

From then on, there were no more dates with Jack's cousin. The one letter I sent her after they'd gone back to Clearwater was returned unopened.

Often Jack, his mother, Sis and I would walk from their place on 42nd St. and Ruby to Tompkins Ice Cream parlor on 24th and Capitol Drive and back, thinking nothing of it. The attractions at Tompkins were low price for a double deck cone, and the variety of flavors they had. Each time we went there, I'd try a different flavor. A blue ice cream called Blue Moon was one of my favorites. We'd talk a lot about all kinds of things, joking around as we went. One evening I was feeling so great I said, "I don't care if I have a short life as long as it's a happy one."

After we got home from watching fireworks at Smith Park one 4th of July evening, Pa and us guys were sitting on the porch when we heard a gosh awful explosion tear the air apart to the southeast of us. Before the echoes died, we were off the porch and running toward the sound.

We got to the source of the blast before the fire

engines reached the place. Harold and I did a double take at the flames coming up through the cracks in the alley behind the house that had exploded. It was the home of our friend Paul Wallner and his mother and dad on the northeast corner of 36th and Hampton Ave. They were standing in the yard in a kind of trance at the shock of their home's explosion.

It didn't take long once the fire department got there to get things under control.

We learned that Paul's dad had gone into the basement to light the hot water heater. Almost as soon as he lit the match, the place blew up, but he escaped without a scratch.

It took some time to rebuild the place, but apparently the gas company had been at fault in the cause, so it picked up the tab for the rebuilding.

A couple of years later, Paul's Dad got their first car. I was over there one Sunday afternoon and was invited to go for a ride with them. Pulling away from the house, his Dad asked, "Where should we go?" It was raining, so just for the heck of it I said, "I wonder if it's raining in Racine." Paul told me afterwards, he couldn't believe his Dad would take me up on it. We got a nice ride to Racine and back, stopping at a small restaurant for coffee and dessert.

One of my stamp collecting friends was Howard Pape who lived in an apartment building near school. I was over there one day with my first hard cover stamp album that had just been used to place my stamps from the soft cover album I'd had. I almost wished I hadn't brought it over there. Howie's mother looked through it, and asked Howie, "Why can't your collection be so well organized?"

Art's Odyssey Unplanned

There were times Eddy Chesnik would ask me to come over and help him with his homework, this for the guy who rarely did his own! Going to his place was almost always an education in its self. Eddy was the youngest of 9 siblings. The next youngest was his brother Rudy, who was also a great guy.

While working on Eddy's homework, an older sister came over to the table, handed Eddy some money, and we walked over to Schwartzman's Drug Store on Hampton and Hopkins. There Eddy bought a package of Modess.

Walking back to Eddy's house, I had to ask. "Eddy, what's that Modess you bought for your sister?" After telling me, "That's because she's having her period." I asked, "What's that got to do with Modess?" The only kinds of period I knew about was the time, the grammar, and the periodical table in chemistry.

Eddy proceeded to inform me the only way he knew how. Using the vernacular, he compared the nocturnal emissions of guy with the menstrual period of girls. Then, before reaching his house, he said, "I gotta take a leak," and did so on the sidewall as we walked.

One evening while doing homework at Eddy's house, his mother walked past, stopping to take a look at the writing we were doing. Turning around she walked back to the living room, and I heard everyone there laughing loudly as she'd said something in Croatian.

Asking Eddy was what so funny made him laugh too. He finally told me, "Ma told the family that after seeing Art's handwriting, she wasn't worried about passing the test to become an American citizen."

Art Schmitz

Not too long after Paul Wallner's new house had been built, Harold, Howie Pape, and I were over there waiting for Paul to finish some chores before going to the Ritz to see a movie. His folks were taking a nap. While waiting we swapped a bunch of locker room jokes.

Seeing Paul at school the next day, he told us his folks had heard all the stories we'd told and we couldn't come over to his house anymore, or he to ours. That lasted a couple of weeks, and after that we were ok to visit again. His folks were from Austria, and his mother was more than happy to clue me in on questions I had about stuff I'd seen on Austrian stamps. His Dad never said much to us.

Feeling really good one summer day, I came into the house and the most delicious smell hit my nose. Sis and Wanny were cooking up a batch of butterscotch. Not being able to resist, I stuck a finger in the liquid cooking in a small pan on the stove.

I made a quick dive for the bathroom, partly because Sis was totally furious, and partly because the stuff was hotter than blazes. Too mad to think, she threw a light bulb at me, that missed and broke into pieces.

The other reason was, after locking the door, to put my finger under the cold water faucet. Almost as soon as the water hit the finger, the butterscotch congealed into a tight sheath on the finger. The pain lasted just a few seconds. I couldn't peel the stuff off my finger, but had no trouble biting into it, and enjoying a real treat as I ate the butterscotch sheath from my finger. I don't know what Sis did with the rest of it, and I didn't really care.

Art's Odyssey Unplanned

Out for a walk one day when I was about 10, I walked on the west side of 37th St. past the second house north of Stark St. There was a small blond headed boy standing on a lower step. Thinking nothing of it, except that I knew he was new to the area, I was surprised when he spat at me. He was even more surprised when I spat a glob right on his face.

That's when his Dad came out, and I thought I was really in for it this time. To my surprise, his Dad thanked me, saying "Maybe that'll teach Billy to stop doing that." It did.

Later on, I wound up walking Billy to Kindergarten on my way to school. He and Eddy Kaupla were the same age and became good friends.

In spite of the age difference, I wound up having some really nice times at Billy Winkleff's house, his mother being especially good with a bunch of kids playing together in their living room, and was always up with suitable refreshments.

Early on during high school days, we started exploring new, to us, ways of having fun. Near Bobby's house on 8th St. was a Lutheran church with a bowling alley in the basement. We'd often watched Bowlers at Marino's Alley in the Plankinton Arcade, but never had done so ourselves.

The church alley, using older boys as pin setters, had the advantage of being cheaper than most of the commercial alleys, and was close to a place we'd be at anyway.

Plus, with Pa along, Bobby, Sis, Harold, and I, we had a full team. None of us had our own bowling balls or shoes but that didn't matter. As time went by, all of our scores began to climb with skill development. Soon we began to explore other, somewhat more expensive alleys like the Comfort Bar on Hopkins St.

Thanks to Jack Gehl, we tried out roller skating at the Riverview Rink at the east end of the North Avenue viaduct. Renting skates to skate to the music of the Wurlitzer organ, I'd thrill to the sound of the music as I glided along on the floor. In a strange sort of way, I had no problem finding good looking girls to skate hand in hand across the floor.

I'd often skate until the late announcement of closing time, and take whoever I'd been skating with to a nearby restaurant for a soda or sundae. One of my more religious friends at school frowned on skating to organ music as he thought that should be reserved for church music, alleging that it was sacrilegious for an organ to be used for anything else.

It wasn't long after the beating I took from Pa for not eating my oatmeal that things changed. Eating and enjoying it was something grownups did. I ate some stuff because the grownups made me do it, but it wasn't anything I enjoyed.

When the Schmitz Grandparents, the Tante, and Bobby lived on 21st and Keefe, we got to know the people living downstairs, Mr. and Mrs. Hayes and their two daughters, who were a little younger than Bobby and me. One Sunday, the Hayes's invited all of us to dinner.

It was a roast beef meal with mashed potatoes, gravy, Jell-O for dessert, and milk for us kids. I'd barely bit into the meat that I felt obligated to pretend to enjoy, when all of a sudden I was shocked with the realization that I'd never, ever, tasted anything that was as good to eat as that meat and everything that went with it!

I wasn't the only one surprised. Pa and Ma sat there with their mouths open when, with all the courtesy I could muster, very politely asked Mrs. Hayes if I could have some more of that great tasting meat. I guess nobody'd ever thought that until then my taste buds had been slow to kick in.

I'd always been intrigued by words. When I was 10, I found that by sending in a fairly large number of the small coupons that came with a pack of Raleigh's cigarettes, I could get my own pocket dictionary.

Pa smoked Lucky Strike, but some of his friends and other people I knew smoked Raleigh's. I may have made a nuisance of myself, but eventually I got enough to send in for my pocket dictionary.

Not long after that I said "ain't" in class. Mrs. Evans said, "Arthur, we don't say words that aren't in the dictionary." After school, I checked the big dictionary and sure enough, ain't wasn't listed.

When I got home I checked my new pocket dictionary and sure enough, there it was, "ain't". I brought it to school the next day, and feeling a sense of great triumph, showed it to Mrs. Evans. "Arthur," she said, "Please read the definition to me." I did. It was, "ain't, an illiterate contraction." "All right, Arthur. Now find the definitions for illiterate and contraction, and read them to yourself." I did, and quietly walked back to my seat, beaten again.

Harry and Irene Walters were a young couple renting that front bedroom. Originally from Nebraska, both of them had daytime jobs. With the way things were going in Europe, I'd race home for lunch, turn on the radio and listen to the latest news.

While eating a sandwich with a cup of coffee I'd hear the Prime Minister of England, or Adolf Hitler addressing his people. If I had some time to spare, I'd play some of Harry and Irene's records on their portable record player.

They were all popular records with a few novelty records in their collection. One of my favorites was "I'm so Sorry for Myself." I could relate to that one. I found myself singing it on my way back to school. "I'm so sorry for myself, I'm so sorry for myself. I'd jump right off from a building tall, but 40 stories is an awful fall. I'm so sorry for myself, I'm so sorry for myself. I'd jump right into the deep blue sea, but nobody'd be there to rescue me, I'm so sorry for myself."

Harry and Irene would often sit in the parlor with us in the evening, but if I listened to some foreign language program, especially the Deutsche Stunde, the German Hour, they'd go back into their room; they felt strongly that it was un-American to go for that foreign stuff.

I was 17 when Ma rented the room to a recently divorced woman and her two small girls. The oldest was 9, and her smaller sister was 5. From somewhere in Illinois, the kids had no sense of any kind of orderly behavior, and it didn't take long for Ma to tell Mrs. Walker she had to find another place.

They left, but it didn't take long before Mrs. Walker came over to offer me a job.

Coming from the very small town in Illinois, she was scared stiff about driving in a big city like Milwaukee.

Art's Odyssey Unplanned

If I'd agree to move in with them, stay with the kids while she worked, and do whatever driving was required, she'd pay me. That was okay with the folks if I wanted to do that, so I did.

Mrs. Walker had a '36 Ford that was easy to drive, so I drove her to the lower flat she'd rented near 22nd and Kilbourn Ave. She had a job as a nurse's aide at a hospital. I'd drive her to work, then drive back to the apartment with the kids.

Every few weeks she'd have to change shifts, so all I had to do when she was on nights, was feed the kids supper, get them to bed, and read or listen to a radio till I went to bed. She'd wake us up when getting back from work, then go to bed, and leave me with the kids to watch while she slept.

The deal was, she'd pay me $10 a week, and I had free use of the car when she was at work. Even when we weren't burning up gas going places, I had the girls pretty well under control; they behaved much better than when they were at our place.

I finally figured out why they'd come to Wisconsin. Mrs. Walker had relatives on a farm several miles west of Milwaukee. Sometimes on a weekend we'd drive out there and stay overnight. Ma would have had a fit if she knew what the setup was out there.

I shared a room with a nephew of Mrs. Walker's who was my age. I slept in my underwear as I did at the apartment, but he slept in the nude. One Sunday morning, he said I should wake up the girls for breakfast. At the apartment, they slept in their under things, but I was surprised to find them both naked when I woke them. The one fringe benefit was a fairly good sized pond on the farm, and the nephew and I'd go skinny dipping there in the evening.

I was beginning to catch on to Mrs. Walker's habits. It seemed as if every two weeks we'd move to a different place, but always in the same general area. It dawned on me that the reason was non-payment of the rent. She was also doing the same thing to me; either giving me a few bucks, or telling me she'd pay me next week.

Going home on my day off, the folks told me they were going up to Peninsula State Park, and could I go up with them. I went back to the apartment, asked for the money she owed me, and was told she couldn't pay me today. I told her, "I quit, but I'll be back for the money."

Two weeks later, back from Door County, I went back to Mrs. Walker's apartment, but they'd moved again. A neighbor who'd done some babysitting for the girls told me where they were.

They were only two blocks away. The oldest girl let me in to find Mrs. Walker sitting on an older man's lap with her arms around him. Seeing me, she said "I can't pay you, and don't bother coming again, 'cause I'm never going to pay you after you left me in the lurch."

Sliding her off his lap, the guy stood up, took out his wallet and gave me $25 and said, "I don't want you bothering this lady again. Goodbye." I didn't waste any time leaving.

Except for one episode when I was 13, I loved everything about the Nicolet Bay campsite at Peninsula. In my trunks on the beach one day, I'd built the most intricate sand structure I'd ever done. It took all morning to do, but it was a detailed masterpiece of a medieval castle with crenellated towers and everything.

While I was trying to figure out how to get Pa and Ma down to see it, another boy about a year younger came over, and with a couple of kicks totally ruined it. Seething with anger, I swatted him on the cheek as hard as I could manage. He took off, bawling his head off. I didn't care. It served him right.

Before I could leave to tell the family what had happened, the kid was back with his father. The man read me the riot act for hitting his son who he said was recovering from mastoid surgery on the side of the head that I'd hit.

After listening to the man, feeling bad that I'd maybe done some serious damage to his son, I explained my reason for hitting the kid. His father looked down and could see what was left of my project.

He was quiet for a moment, and then, before the kid could say or do anything, he swatted the kid on his butt as hard as he could and I wondered if he was ever going to stop. You could have heard the kid's screams in Sturgeon Bay 30 miles away before they walked off the beach to their camp site. I never saw them again.

One year, instead of camping, we rented a cabin in Fish Creek and took Grandma and Grandpa Hill with us. As usual, Pa rented a row boat we could use for either fishing or just rowing around. I caught some really big perch off the pier.

One afternoon, while Pa and Grandpa were drinking their Golden Drops beer at the tavern, Grandpa gave me a dime to put in the slot machine.

I lucked out when it spit out 80 cents. Grandpa was ecstatic.

I knew enough about the odds that I was about to quit while we were ahead, but Grandpa insisted, and almost forcibly made me feed the machine the whole 80 cents, completely mystified as to why we didn't get any more money back.

One afternoon, with Grandpa's dog Tiny on the back seat of the boat, I rowed out on the little bay of the Fish Creek harbor. Seeing a seagull sitting on the water, I steered the boat so the back was facing the bird.

Pa was walking with Grandpa Hill on the pier next to the bay when Tiny spotted the bird. The seagull was in the air before Tiny hit the water. Grandpa Hill saw his dog hit the water, and scared stiff that the mutt was going to drown, went nuts on the pier screaming and cussing me out for letting that happen. He didn't know dogs were pretty good swimmers, and we weren't that far out that Tiny couldn't get to the shore, which he did. I took my time getting back to the cabin, and by then Pa'd taken Grandpa for a draft of Golden Drops.

Grandpa Hill told Pa he'd like to someday go back to see the farm he worked on when he first came to this country. It was near Clinton, Iowa. I don't know where Harold and Sis were that weekend, but I was delegated to dog sit for Tiny while they were gone.

It was about as close as I ever came to being bored. There wasn't much I wanted to listen to on the radio. I couldn't take in a movie, and except when I took Tiny for a walk on the leash, I wasn't getting a lot of exercise for the energy I had.

Scrounging around in places I'd never looked in before, I found a bottle of some kind of liquor I'd not seen before. That required some sampling, and I loved the flavor.

I figured I couldn't drink too much of the stuff, 'cause Danny'd be sure to notice, but I did enjoy some every once in a while.

Grandma and Grandpa Hill loved to have folks over for Saturday evening parties, and there was often a gathering of mutual friends of the folks, and neighbors, usually enjoying their beer, etc. in the fixed-up basement.

On one of those party nights, I was upstairs with Tiny. I poured a little beer into a sauce dish I put on the floor. Sure enough, Tiny checked it out and lapped it up. I put a little more in the dish, and he really went at it, looking up at me, begging for more. I gave him some more.

After a bit, I heard Grandpa call Tiny. He wanted to show him to some folks downstairs. Tiny responded, going to the stairs, promptly falling down the steps to the party. I decided this was a good time to take a long walk in the evening air.

We sometimes celebrated Thanksgiving at the Hill house. One year, Pa and Danny went to a nearby tavern a few nights before Thanksgiving. Ma and Grandma, ticked because they hadn't been asked to go along, decided to fix the men.

They found an empty case of beer bottles, and filled them with a concoction of old coffee and soapy water, leaving it to me to cap the bottles. Then, hiding a full case of the real thing, they put the loaded case in its' place.

On Thanksgiving Day, we enjoyed a terrific turkey dinner with all the other good stuff and homemade pumpkin pie for dessert. While the women cleaned up in the kitchen, us guys went into the living room. To me it was funny to hear the two women talking about how much harder each worked than the other one.

It wasn't long before I was asked to bring up a couple bottles of beer for Danny and Pa. Danny always drank right from the bottle, but Pa always poured his into a glass.

Pa immediately noticed the problem with the beer in his glass, but Danny, taking a great swig, almost threw the bottle while sputtering at the mix in his mouth. The women had heard, and worked hard at stifling their laughing. It took a few minutes, but I was delegated to go downstairs and bring up a couple of bottles of the real stuff.

As time went by, our family and Kaupla's became close friends. One Sunday afternoon, each family using its own car, we all drove to see some friends of Kaupla's in Watertown, about 45 miles west of Milwaukee. After having lunch with the Watertown friends, Wilbur, Pa, and Ed Kaupla went to a nearby tavern.

When they hadn't come back by supper time, we went ahead and ate. Grandma

Baker had come along, and as the women wondered about the men, Grandma didn't help when she talked a blue streak about all the terrible things that she thought had already happened; she made it clear she didn't want to spend the night in Watertown. Ma finally told her to quit being such a crepe hanger.

The guys didn't get back till well after 8 o'clock,

and all of them were stewed to the gills, barely able to walk. The question of how Pa and Ed Kaupla were going to drive back in their condition was worrying.

With everyone determined to get back to Milwaukee, a trial solution was worked out. I rode shotgun with Mr. Kaupla, as did Ma with Pa. I figured Ma was doing the same thing I was. Whenever it looked as if Mr. Kaupla was veering too far to one side of the two-lane highway or the other, I'd squirt into his mouth from the several slices of lemon I had in my hand. It seemed to work. At least we all got back in one piece.

Just as Bobby was with us camping at Nicolet Bay, Wanny often came along. We all tried to get tans on as much of our bodies as possible. One hot summer day, Sis and Wanny were laying on a blanket, the back straps of their bra's off, so the stripe wouldn't show on their tan.

That was too much of a temptation for us. All three of us guys tried everything we could think of to say or do, that would get them to at least sit up. Not only didn't it work, but we got in trouble with the folks when they heard about it. They already knew what Wanny's Dad thought of any guys involved with his daughter.

One afternoon, me rowing the boat, I had Sis and Wanny as passengers. They asked if I'd row them to Horseshoe Island, a little less than a mile out from Nicolet Bay. We got there, beached the boat and started walking inland.

We ran like bats out of hell to get in the boat and get away as fast as we could. We hadn't known there was a seagull rookery on the island, and although not actually being touched by any of the birds, they'd swooped too close for comfort down on us, screaming loudly at this threat to their nests.

Harold and I were downtown one Saturday afternoon. Pointing to a yellow #19 streetcar on 3rd St., I said, "Look, the front of that streetcar, looks like the face of a bloodhound." Harold stopped walking, saying, "You go ahead, I don't want to be seen with a crazy nut."

By the time I was a senior, that $5 Victrola Ma'd got when I was 12 had played its last record. After all those years of heavy use, the turntable would turn, but much slower than the 78 rpms required to turn a record so it sounded good.

There was only one thing to do, and that was take it apart and see if I could fix it. I had unexpected help. This was right up Harold's alley. It took some doing to separate the mechanism from the wooden casing. We spent several days after school and evenings trying to make it work again, but the operating spring was totally shot. The whole thing went out in the trash.

That was why, when the folks asked what I wanted for a graduation present, I had an easy answer. I went to Gimbels with Ma to pick it out. It was the new Philco Combination Radio and Phonograph, the latter being the main part of my choice.

They both were operated electrically. No more winding up to play a record. The radio had shortwave reception as well as standard, but it was the features of the record player that had my special interest.

No more keeping a supply of new needles to play records with minimum needle noise. The Philco used a very small light to reflect the permanent stylus's movement on the grooves of the record, converting it to a virtually noise-free record play. It was called a beam-of-light operation.

We got 5 free records with the Philco, but Ma wasn't happy with one of my title choices. It was the popular Georgia Tech pep song, "I'm a ramblin' wreck from Georgia Tech and a helluva engineer."

At graduation time, the Nichol's were living with us. They had a son, Robert, in 4th grade. Partly because of my taste in music, Harold got along with them better than I did. Mr. Nichols was a delivery truck driver for Omar Bakery.

I was jealous when summer came and they invited Harold to spend vacation time with them at a cabin on a lake up north for 2 weeks.

Harold and Robert came home with great tans, and stories about the fish they caught. But the best story was the one about coming up on a group of girls skinny dipping on the other side of the lake, and being asked to join them! Harold would have if Robert hadn't been in the boat with him.

Dishes were a constant problem. The three of us did them together, and there was always an argument about who was going to do what. I preferred washing them because I'd be done first, but so did Harold and Sis for the same reason. Putting them away wasn't bad either, but I didn't care much for drying them. We weren't exactly quiet about our preferences.

Occasionally one of us would drop a dish, breaking it, and Ma'd yell at us, accusing us of breaking dishes on purpose because we didn't want to do them. We rarely had to do the good dishes reserved for special occasions.

A lot of times I'd be told to set the table for lunch or supper. We had a set of knives with crummy looking yellow handles. The knives were so dull they wouldn't cut through Jell-O, so I'd slice the non-cutting sharp edge across the palm of my hand. I did that setting the table for lunch one day, and I saw bloody cuts across my palm. Pa hadn't said he'd sharpened the knives.

Eggs were a common food item, not just for breakfast. Ma'd fix one of my favorite meals, two poached eggs on toast in milk, hot and served in a soup dish, often for supper.

One Sunday morning, when Grandma Baker was there, I asked Pa, why do some eggs have white shells, and others have brown shells? He explained that the brown shelled eggs came from roosters, and the white came from hens.

Grandma, basically a farm lady, yelled at Pa. "You'll make those kids the laughing stock with the other kids at school! Pa was full of stuff like that, and we knew it.

Winters didn't mean we were deprived of our Sunday outings with Pa. Out in all kinds of weather walking his mail route, he still took us out on winter Sundays.

We were still in grade school, when one wintry Sunday we went to McKinley Beach. It was the first time I'd seen Lake Michigan frozen solid as far as I could see. As usual, Bobby stayed on shore, but Harold and I got a thrill out of walking out on the ice with Pa, and climbing over huge chunks of ice sticking up in all kinds of weird shapes above the surface of the lake.

Art's Odyssey Unplanned

One of my favorite places near McKinley park was Maitland Field, not a field at all, but the location of a seaplane area near the Coast Guard station. There were a couple of planes based there, and it was always my hope that I'd see one take off while I was there to watch, but it never happened. The intriguing thing about the planes was the positioning of their propellers above the fuselage instead of on the front.

On my 11th Thanksgiving, the whole relation was at our house for Thanksgiving dinner in the early afternoon. Some of the grownups were betting on who'd eat the most mashed potatoes; Grandma Baker or Bobby.

After the pumpkin pie dessert, and after checking with Bobby and Harold, I asked Pa if he'd take us for a walk. Pa, just as well satisfied to escape having to do any of the cleanup, asked where we wanted to walk to.

"Could we walk to the airport?" "Yeah, we can do that." Although there wasn't any snow on the ground, the air was a crisp cold.

Pa knew when we said "airport" that we were talking about Curtis-Wright, and not the county airport on the other side of town. It took us about an hour to hike the distance, but we enjoyed the walk.

When we got there, we first went to visit an old lodge buddy of Pa's living with his wife and two daughters on the north side of the airport. After a short stay, Bobby, Harold, and I walked over to the airport, checking out aircraft before Bobby and Harold decided to go back to Pa's friend's house.

On my own now, I began to explore the hangars that weren't locked. There were a few men around, but they paid no attention to me. They didn't say I couldn't when they'd see me climb into the cockpits of small planes.

But, the best was when I got into a Ford Tri-Motor passenger plane. First checking out the wicker work passenger seat, I got to the pilot's seat, and in my mind, became a pilot taking off into the air.

I could see it was getting dark, so I walked back to Pa and the guys. Before long we began the hike home eastward along Silver Spring Road.

About halfway home, we told Pa we needed to use a bathroom. Pa told us "go into that field. There isn't any traffic so nobody'll see you." Harold and I did, emptied our bladders and rejoined Pa and Bobby.

Getting to Hopkins St. there was a bus at the Silver Spring Road end of the #59 route. Bobby asked Pa if we could take the bus the rest of the way. Pa said, "You guys wanted to go for a walk, so we're walking," and we walked the rest of the way home. We barely got in the front door when everybody held their noses. Bobby should have gone into the field with us. He hadn't made it.

As I got bigger, I found new ways of using old toys. I had an old set of blocks, about 2" by 2" that were meant to be educational with numbers and letters of the alphabet on them. One evening after supper, I got Harold to help me piling the blocks on top of each other in a corner of our room. Eventually using a wooden chair to put the blocks higher than we otherwise could reach, we got our tower as high as we could make it.

I got down off the chair. Once on the floor, I bent down and pulled out the bottom block, bringing the rest of them down with a gosh awful racket that was music to our ears.

We got an unexpected dividend. Ma charged in our door, fully expecting to see some kind of bloody mess in our room. That we hadn't expected, but it set the stage for doing it again in the not too distant future. A week or so later, we repeated the action, scaring the daylights out of Ma working in the kitchen, but her mistake was not telling us not to do that again.

Grandpa Baker wasn't much of a talker when he was at our house, but he seemed to like me. I liked him too. He chewed tobacco, and taking me up to the attic with him, he'd give me some to chew. I felt like a grownup.

One afternoon, chewing together, I had to cough and swallowed the wad I had in my mouth, forcing myself to vomit all over the place. Crying, I ran downstairs to get cleaned up. We never did that again.

Harold sometimes slept at Bobby's house with me at Grandma Baker's place, but I don't think Sis ever spent the night with any of her girlfriends. On the other hand, I slept at Kenny Isaacson's place when they lived on our side of the street, and Paul Van Luven's house on Hampton Avenue just west of the railroad tracks.

The first time there, I didn't get much sleep listening to the switching operations going on during the night. There were other summer nights that were so hot, we slept in the minimum of clothing; fans didn't help much.

I didn't make any brownie points at Grandma Schmitz's house either with fans on hot summer days. I'd take strips of paper, and let the fan blades slice them into pieces that flew all over the place after I stuck them into the fan.

At Bobby's house in August of 1935, I had a splitting headache, a rarity for me to have any kind of headache. Bobby and I weren't getting along too well either. Tante Margaret had the radio on, but nobody was really listening to it.

Whatever music was playing got interrupted by an announcer saying that Wiley Post and Will Rogers had been killed when their plane crashed at Point Barrow, Alaska.

I wouldn't have paid much attention to it, but Will Rogers was one of my favorite columns in the paper, and I loved his movies. What I couldn't believe was that the surprising news had wiped out my headache! I felt great and down at the same time.

I was never a great puzzle fan, but to create some semblance of harmony, Tante Margaret offered to pay Bobby and I a dime each if we'd do a jig-saw puzzle she had. By the time we finished the puzzle, I'd had it. If it had taken any more time, I would have quit working on it.

Not too long after that, for some reason or other, or no reason at all, I told the Tante, "You're so ugly, your face would stop a clock." She got really mad at me, and told me in no uncertain terms to apologize to her. "I won't do that, and you can't make me," was my reply. I couldn't admit that I had no idea what apologize meant, and I wasn't going to ask her.

I went downtown on a Friday night after graduation. I got on a Rapid Transit train headed for Waukesha. I had my 8th grade teacher, Mrs. Ollwell's address. Getting off the two-car train after riding in the left front seat of the first car, I walked up a hill to her home.

She very nicely introduced me to her husband, offered a hot chocolate, and invited me to sit down for a visit. I wound up staying there for a couple of hours. We'd got along very well when I was in her class, and that seemed to continue.

I finally left her home, walking back down the hill to the Rapid Transit depot. I had to wait quite some time for the train to return to Milwaukee. Once on board, I made sure I sat in the same seat going back.

From that seat I could see the rails, signal lights, and platforms at the various possible stops. The engineer had the same view from his enclosure on the right front of the train.

We'd made quite a few stops coming out, but going back on an almost empty train, and nobody waiting on any of the platforms, I was thrilled at the speed we ran on the return trip. It didn't take much to feel as if I was the engineer. We ran like a bat out of hell!

By the time I got back to Milwaukee, the streetcar and bus lines were running on what we called the owl schedule, that is every hour instead of the 15 minutes or so of the normal operating hour schedule. Pa and I had an understanding. The next day he'd ask, "What time did you get home last night." If I said "early," he knew it was before midnight. If I said, "late," he knew it was after midnight. Neither Pa or Ma waited up for us when we'd be out for the evening.

One thing about Tante Margaret, she seemed to understand my interest in things foreign. For my 12th birthday she gave me a slim book that I came to cherish for a long time afterwards. It had easily read descriptions of the lives and customs of a lot of different people in different countries, and was profusely illustrated with color pictures of young people in their native clothing.

After Grandpa Hill got to know me, he gave me copies of advertising publications he got at work, showing a lot of color pictures of buses and streetcars being used in other cities. He also let me use some of his tools in the basement workshop he had; especially the grinding wheels for sharpening tools, knives, etc.

Ma was scared stiff that we might hurt ourselves with anything sharp around the house. When Mrs. Parr suggested letting me use scissors to cut out stuff from the paper, she told Ma she could get scissors without sharp points for me to use.

One morning after staying the night at Grandma Schmitz's house, we were having sliced bananas with milk for breakfast. When I asked Grandma to slice my bananas for me, she said, "Here, I'll show you how, and then you can do it yourself. Your Mama will be so proud of you when you do it at home."

That did it. I'd never really watched Ma do it, but I watched Grandma, and then did it myself. I didn't have to wait till I got home. I was proud of myself for being able to do that.

I often saw Tante Margaret doing office type work at home, so one semester I decided to take book keeping. Mr. Ashcraft was the teacher, a nice enough man, but I had real problems distinguishing between debits and credits, among other items of the course vocabulary.

After I'd handed in an attempt at the homework

assignment we'd had, Mr. Ashcraft came down the aisle, handed my work back to me without a grade at the top and said, "This is a cataclysmic catastrophe," before going back to his desk at the front of the room. He, Ma, and I had a conference, and I wound up dropping the course. The weird thing about it was that from the time I'd learned to talk, I had a real love of words, but mixing words and figures was another story for me.

The two of us were doing dishes one day, and not knowing what got into me, I started talking to Harold in the most insulting and nasty ways I could think of, to the point where, unable to do anything in rebuttal, he broke down in tears.

I'd thought I wanted to bug him, but hadn't meant to really hurt him to the point of making him cry. I would have understood if he'd stopped doing the dishes, and started beating up on me, but I hadn't seen this coming. I couldn't do it right away, but later on I managed to let him know I'd been that mean to him, and didn't really mean to hurt him like that.

It seemed as if older people, and those much younger than I, liked me, but people somewhat older than I was didn't. A good example was when Kenny gave Harold the boat he'd made. Another time, Lawrence, Uncle Ollie, and Aunt Clara's oldest son gave Harold a really neat solid wood model of an airplane he'd made. I was burning with jealousy. I was 9 at the time.

A few months later, I was mad as I could be at Harold for some reason or another, and knowing he'd beat me in a physical fight, I tried to figure out how I could get even.

Going into our bedroom I saw Harold's plane on a shelf in the closet. I took it down, fully intending to completely destroy it.

Putting the plane on the bed while I thought of just how I'd ruin it, I looked at it for a bit, and then quietly picked it up and put it back on the shelf. I'd come to the place where I'd developed something of a conscience, and knew there'd be no way I could make amends for what I'd wanted to do. I could never have repaired or replaced the plane.

One of my favorite streetcar rides was the #10 across the Wells St. viaduct running across the Menomonee River valley below. It was different from the Wisconsin Ave. viaduct a block south. That was only vehicular and pedestrian traffic, while the Wells St. viaduct was a bridge for streetcars only.

Going either way, the motorman usually went as fast as possible from one end to the other. At the west end, some cars kept going west into Wauwatosa, while others turned south to West Allis. Usually going just for the ride, unless going to the Fair Grounds in West Allis, I didn't much care which way it went.

I'd left a New Year's Eve party in Wauwatosa after 3 o'clock the morning of New Year's Day. We came to a dead stop half way across the viaduct. Some drunk had tried to drive west across the streetcar tracks only structure, before trying to make a U-turn in the middle of the bridge.

Knowing we were going to be there for a while, I fell asleep, not waking up until I felt the streetcar moving again. The sun was just coming up, so I had no idea of how they got the car off the viaduct, but the motorman made speed once we got going. I got home in time for breakfast with the family.

I graduated on January 27th, 1942. Three days before that we were called to the Convalescent Home on North Avenue where Grandma Schmitz had just died. We'd been close through the years.

It was the first time I'd seen a dead person before the body was served by an undertaker. Grandma almost looked as if she'd answer a question if one had asked her. I knew Pa must have felt something, but he didn't show any signs of tears, crying, or grief.

By the next day, Grandma was laid out at the Rasch Funeral Home. Most of the details of graduation had been worked out, so I was available to fill in as the chauffeur, taking friends and relatives to and from the funeral home.

Often there was room so Harold and Bobby rode with me. With a lot of the people living in Bay View, we were able to take full advantage of what we called the south side speedway, South Chase Ave. I got no tickets.

One of the best jobs I had after graduation was being a bus boy at Boston Store's 6th floor restaurant. Pretty hard at first, it took some learning before I was anything like efficient. Besides bussing dishes, etc. from the tables after they'd been used, I was supposed to supply the kitchen with stuff from the refrigerator.

I had to learn names of different kinds of meat I'd never heard of before, like one called Mortadella, a kind of ham by the looks of it. I didn't mind being on my feet most of the day; there was enough variety in the things I did to keep me too occupied to worry about it.

Besides the $25 a week I was getting, the girls in the kitchen often had a soda or sundae waiting for me. Some of them were more than willing to go out with me in the evening. We had some great times, especially those evenings I could get Pa to let me use the car, which gave us some privacy.

With the money I was making, I could afford the gas, dancing at the Eagles Club, bowling, taking in a movie, and having something good for a treat before taking her home. Although being fairly talkative, I never said much about my evenings to the family. As long as I got home in one piece, Ma and Pa weren't worried.

It was one of the more lasting jobs I had, going for several months before I was told my services were no longer required. The boss gave me an earful after I slipped on something slippery on the floor, and losing my balance spilled most of a glass of water I'd removed from a table on to a well-dressed woman sitting at another table. Plus he'd been unhappy about the costs of the treats the girls in the kitchen were giving me.

All three of us often had our differences, but there were times we enjoyed each other's company. Our friends, the Kaupla's moved to a house down around 18th Street and Atkinson Ave. but we stayed in touch.

One Saturday afternoon with nothing much else to do, Sis and I walked the couple of miles from our house to Kaupla's. We talked about all kinds of stuff on our way there.

After visiting for a couple of hours, we started the walk back and, being fairly well talked out, holding hands and swinging our arms in unison we started

Art's Odyssey Unplanned

to sing the simple songs we knew, as well as some we'd heard others sing, like "99 bottles of beer on the wall." Finally getting home in time for supper, we had a good appetite for whatever Ma was going to put on the table.

There was one item that never failed to get my attention at the Museum. That was the huge section of pull out frames housing the stamp collection one of Milwaukee's great business people had donated to the Museum.

In the beginning, I had no idea the value of the collection, but I was endlessly fascinated by the incredible variety of postage stamps from all over the world that could be seen by a kid like myself. I spent hours looking at the figures of kings, queens, and other famous people, and the strange array of foreign country names and money values.

I was 9 and Harold a year or so younger when we were both bed ridden with Chicken Pox. Both of us were utterly miserable, and subject to the orders of Grandma Baker because Ma found it expedient to be gone a lot, Sis was in school and too young to be of any help, and Pa was at work.

Grandma, being the sympathetic soul that she was, finally had it with our yelling out. Coming into our room, she told us, "You guys settle down and shut up, or I'll send you to the pest house before your Ma gets home."

Totally shocked into silence, we were too scared to ask for details about this pest house that Grandma knew about. We knew that grownups often thought of kids as pests, but we didn't know there was a special house for pests. It wasn't until years later that we learned what then was Southview Hospital, a facility for kids with diseases like Infantile Paralysis, had originally been for illnesses like Smallpox.

All the kids' diseases weren't like Chicken Pox. I think I was the only one of us, naturally, who got the Mumps when I was 8. When it was known that someone had one of the contagious diseases like that, someone from the Health Department put a conspicuous sign on the front of the house.

I took full advantage of that. I had the Mumps, but felt really good, except for the painless swelling on my neck. The weather was nice, so I could go out a lot. I didn't much care for Tommy, one of the two kids living in the house south of ours.

When he'd be outside, I'd (against all the rules) go over there and tease him. He knew I had something bad, but when he'd come near me to fight, I'd quietly go back to my side of the lot, and he didn't dare follow me; not with that sign on the door.

Our families really didn't get along too well. Mr. Berbaum, obviously of German descent, and Mrs. Berbaum of Irish, were Roman Catholic and we were, if anything, Protestant. The real rub was, as Mrs. Berbaum said more than once, was that Pa had a steady job, times were bad, and Mr. Berbaum, a self-employed carpenter had to scrounge for a living.

I'd always liked little kids, and after Tommy's sister Betty was born, I'd often go over there to see the baby. After I'd been in their bedroom looking at the cute little thing in her crib, I went home.

Later that day, Mrs. Berbaum came to our house screaming that I'd stolen $5 she'd had on the dresser in the bedroom where the baby was. Ma called me, and when I got in the kitchen, asked me for the money I'd taken. I said, "I hadn't taken any money."

Ma pulled me to her, and pulled my pants pockets out, with nothing there, but a handkerchief. That was bad enough, but I felt completely crushed and betrayed when Ma got her purse, and gave Mrs. Berbaum $5. I couldn't know that Ma'd do almost anything to keep peace with others.

A few days later, out of the blue, Mr. Berbaum called Harold, Sis, and I over to take us for a ride to Bill's grocery store on Fairmount Ave., a little more than a block away. There, he told us to pick out any kind of candy we wanted, and he'd pay for it. Naturally, we took him up on his offer, and rode home loaded with pockets and hands full of candy.

Because of Grandpa Schmitz suffering from sugar diabetes, that was something Ma or Pa would never do; subject us kids to the dangers of getting diabetes from eating sweets. Ma and Pa finally found out the reason for the treats. Berbaum's had found the $5 I was accused of stealing on the bedroom floor blown there by the wind from an open window. That didn't change the way I felt about Ma not believing me when I'd been accused.

The inconsistency of Ma's concerns about sugar diabetes was that, while we couldn't get candy and sweets from the store, we ate all we could of Ma's homemade great tasting pies, cakes, and other sweet stuff, like 2 spoons of sugar in the coffee I drank.

Early on, I'd begged to be allowed to drink coffee like the grownups, instead of the milk I was served. Ma asked the doctor about that, and his suggestion was, "Give him the milk, but add a little coffee to it, so it looks like coffee." That worked, although once I was able to serve myself it became a case of mostly coffee with a little milk added with 2 spoons of sugar. I got my share of milk in any of the cereals I had for breakfast.

We often had oatmeal for breakfast, but sometimes we had boxed cereals of one kind or another. Often this was a result of radio program advertising. Rice Krispies was a favorite of mine because I liked the "snap, crackle, and pop" sounds as milk was added. General Mills was the sponsor of the "Singing Lady" program advertising the cereal. I enjoyed hearing her sing in connection with the stories she told in the program.

Harold was even guiltier with his insistence on Ma buying Wheaties because of his radio idol, Jack Armstrong, the all-American boy. He was much more intense about that than I was.

I actually had two favorite programs. The other one was about an older boy, Jimmy Allen, and his adventures with planes, sponsored by Skelly gasoline. There wasn't a Skelly gas station in miles of us, so Pa was under no pressure to get that kind of gas.

One weekend after graduation, Jack Langtry and I went to Chicago. He'd finally managed to get in touch with the father he hadn't seen for years. Staying at the Y on 12th and Wabash, we met his father on a street corner in the Loop.

It didn't take long to understand why Jack's mother had divorced him. He'd had a few too many before we got there. A short, skinny guy, not dressed very well, he spent most of the time talking about his unbeatable system for winning bets on the races. Stopping for breath as he talked, I butted in, saying "Mr. Langtry, in other words, you've developed an algebraic system." Thrilled, he slapped me on the back, and told Jack, "I like your friend, he understands me." We didn't stay there much longer. After we left, Jack told me. "I don't care if I never see him again."

Before graduation, Bobby, Harold, and I'd often go to football games at the Rufus King High School stadium where both of our schools played. Bobby was going to North Division High School.

If North was playing, we'd purposely sit on the opposing team's side, and somewhere along the line, we'd belt out: "Gefilte fish, Gefilte fish, veer da boyss from Nort Divish!" After which we'd high tail it over to the north side of the stadium. North Division and Washington High School had a larger percentage of Jewish students than any of the other Milwaukee High Schools.

At Custer, one of my best friends was Andy Petak, a Jewish kid. Seeing him a while after graduation, he said, "You know Art why Mrs. Royal was harder on us than anyone else? I told him, "I didn't think she was hard on us? "I didn't think so either at the time, but looking back, I think it was obvious. We were the two most intelligent kids in the class."

We laughed together as we recalled going down the steps at Custer in our senior year and commenting, "Gee the freshmen are small this year." We'd forgotten that was us four years ago.

We were walking with Pa on one of our Sunday

expeditions downtown when I saw an older man, bleary eyed and bent over, picking up a small butt of what was left of a cigarette next to the sidewalk. I swore to myself, I was never going to let myself get into such a sorry state as that.

On another occasion, Harold and I spotted a $5 bill on the sidewalk, but he beat me to it. I lucked out a few weeks later, finding a ring with an opal, my birthstone set in it.

Miss O'Connell was the teacher of our Junior High Geography class. She assigned us a major project of creating a Wisconsin Work Book that would take us most of the semester to complete. It involved a huge amount of research to find and compile the statistics of all kinds of agricultural, industrial, and other elements of Wisconsin's economic output.

After taking in the full meaning of the assignment, I leaned over to whisper to my friend Herbert Schuster, "I'm gonna save my workbook and give it to my son so he won't have to endure this torture."

Miss O'Connell said, "Arthur, if what you had to say to Herbert was so important, I think you should share it with the whole class, so stand up and tell us what you said."

I did so, but almost immediately I was told to sit down without finishing. Miss O'Connell was shocked at the idea of her students even thinking about having offspring and all that it implied.

Thanks to the Henty books I'd read about the British in Afghanistan, and a more recent book by Lowell Thomas, the movie news commentator about the country, doing a report on Afghanistan was a much easier assignment for me.

Art's Odyssey Unplanned

Miss O'Connell was very unhappy about the earlier repeal of Prohibition. She was very clear that when she traveled, she'd tell people she was from Waukesha, Wisconsin. When asked where that was, she'd say, "About 90 miles northwest of Chicago," instead of 21 miles west of Milwaukee. That way she wouldn't have to be associated with a city known for its breweries.

After gaining the freedom of using buses and streetcars by myself, I became a guide for out of town visitors to our family who wanted to tour the various breweries in Milwaukee. I enjoyed that. We'd get a tour of the brewery, and often a free lunch washed down with freshly brewed beer. Not too crazy about the taste of beer then, I didn't mind getting a free soft drink instead.

I had Mr. Showers again for the 2nd semester of Biology. We had the largest aquarium I'd ever seen outside of the huge aquarium in Chicago. Some kid brought in a small northern pike for the aquarium, and another kid brought in a bunch of very small bullhead as bait.

We got an up-close view of how nature works. In less than an hour the northern was the sole occupant of the aquarium, but it had been fun watching it eat the bullheads.

I'd been too sick to be in school for the Biology final exam, but was there for the final of one of my other classes where I had to take the exam. Mr. Showers came to the door of the room, and guiding me into the hallway, asked me a few questions from the course which I had no trouble answering correctly, so that was my Biology final.

Harold and I were involved in building model airplanes. Using exacto knives to work on the balsa wood that shaped the frame of the fuselage, wings, and tail assembly had to be done with care. Then came the assembly process using a smelly glue.

We weren't perfectionists about most things, but for our models we were. One cold winter evening, I thought of a way to get rid of a model we'd finished, but didn't fill the perfect slot.

We went up to the attic, opened the rear window, wound up the rubber band that powered the plane, and just before letting it fly out the window, I let a match to it, and let it fly. That's when we heard a scream in the back yard!

Pa'd just parked the car in a snow cleared space in the yard after he and Ma'd been shopping. Ma'd just got out of the car when she saw this flaming object coming out of the attic window.

When we saw Ma running toward the house, we closed the window and ran downstairs, getting in the kitchen just about the same time Ma came in the house. We got an earful, but that was it.

Ma had lived in Chicago, working as a Western Union telegraph operator when she and Pa were dating. Now, Pa having an unexpected week off, she asked him to take her and us kids to Chicago to meet some of the people she'd known back then.

We stayed at a hotel on Montrose. Most of those people were no longer there, so Ma and Sis went shopping, using the L, buses, and streetcars like Pa did with Harold and me. We spent a lot of time visiting all the railroad stations. One day we went out to the Armour Company stockyards. We saw stuff I was glad we didn't know in advance that we were going to see. I think I would have figured out some way of backing out.

We went to a huge room, spotlessly clean. We stood on a kind of elevated balcony across from a platform of stainless steel. A man in a white coat stood near the right end of it, holding in his hand a fairly long blade with a sort of hook on the end.

There was a kind of conveyor running above the platform, and hung from it was a pig, it's head down. With one quick stroke of his blade, there was a huge gush of blood pouring from the pig's neck. The man had cut its jugular and the pig was dead.

In another similar setting, it was a cow that had been knocked out as it hung down from another conveyor system. This time, the man with the blade slit open its stomach and a gosh awful looking mess of its innards poured out on the platform. Torn between my curiosity and my aversion to seeing animals killed and bleeding, I held my hands in front of my eyes, peeking between my fingers. After the slaughter facility, we saw sausages being made, and were given a light lunch with Armour meat products.

In Miss Kusta's English class the next week I volunteered to read Carl Sandburg's poem *Chicago*. The class was stunned as, recalling my experience at Armours, I put some real feeling into my reading. Miss Kusta gave a rare in front of the class compliment on my reading.

Not too long after that, Eddy Chesnik and I, one evening, rode the buses to the east side, not knowing we were going to have to walk as far as we did to get to Columbia Hospital. Our mission was to visit Miss

Kusta. All we knew was that she was ill, and in the hospital. Although surprised to see us, we actually had a really pleasant visit with her before visiting hours were over.

She hadn't said we couldn't, but we never told anyone else in our class that we'd visited her. We didn't want them to think we were teacher's pet or anything.

Sophomore boys could take a boys cooking class as an elective course. Most of us who signed up did so because Miss Schlondrop was the youngest and best looking woman teacher in the school.

The class was generally pretty low key. Most of the stuff we made were bakery goods of one kind or another that we were able to eat in class when it was done.

There was a small library in the room that we could use while waiting for our efforts to finish baking. A few of us found, in a brown covered book, material about the growth elements of boys and girls. Puberty was illustrated with black and white full length frontal nudity of a fifteen-year-old boy and girl with just a black line across their eyes.

Ma, skeptical at first, was really happy when I helped with the pumpkin pies at Thanksgiving that year. In the cooking class, I'd learned how to sprinkle brown sugar on the top of a ready to eat pumpkin pie, put it under the gas flame of the stove for a few minutes, and bring it out with a caramelized top that tasted really good.

We were appalled later that semester when a substitute took over the class for a week, but completely disenchanted when Miss Schlondrop returned as a Mrs. Something or other. The class just wasn't the same after that.

The first summer after I joined the Boy Scouts, Pa drove me to Indian Mound, the Boy Scout camp on Silver Lake in Waukesha County, for a week of my first camping experience without the family. It took some getting used to, but I loved it.

There was never a dull moment, but we had time to do things, or not, by ourselves too. Besides sharing a tent with several other guys the same age or a little older, we went on hikes in the woods that made up a large part of the camp; often in the evening singing songs that didn't make a lot of sense, but were fun to sing - like the Boy Scout motto, repeated over and over again, "Be prepared, prepared, prepared, the motto of a true scout."

Another one we sang often was, "If you wanna be a Badger, just come along with me, by the bright shining light, by the light of the moon," sung repeatedly. I didn't know what a Badger was and didn't care, but it was fun to sing.

The hardest thing for me was getting used to a bathroom with nothing separating the flush toilets from each other. It took me awhile to get used to having bowel movements with no privacy.

I was back at Indian Mound the next summer. My friend Gerald Renn, a member of Troop 5, wanted to go to Indian Mound. His father, who insisted Gerald call him Mr. Renn, would pay the cost, if Gerald could find a way to get there and back, so he rode along with us there and back a week later.

The second summer there was even better than the first one. There was a pastor's son in our tent, and he knew more sexy stories than all the rest of us when we'd swap them before going to sleep after lights out. During the day we'd get some of the new guys to run naked around the tent and then have their picture taken without any film in the camera.

There was a decent beach, and we did a lot of swimming. There were also row boats, canoes, some war canoes as they were called, and a few small sail boats - all of which got regular use.

One weekday we all boarded the war canoes in full scout uniform. We paddled across the lake, beached the canoes, and in formation marched a few miles into Oconomowoc. There, standing in formation, we were in a great position to watch James Farley, the Postmaster General, smash a can of Carnation Condensed Milk to christen and dedicate the brand-new Oconomowoc Post Office.

The ceremony didn't last long, and then it was back to the beach in a casual walk, boarding the canoes, and paddling our way across the lake back to camp. It wasn't long after that when we had supper. The tents were pretty quiet fairly early that evening.

One of the guys from our troop got sent home in the middle of the week. He was into Golf and brought his clubs along to the camp. During some free time, he practiced his swing on the toads that were all over the place. Some of the rest of us would catch them with our hands and play with them for a while before letting them go. Nobody got any warts on their hands.

One of the leaders saw him. He was ordered to get his things together and wait in the camp office until someone from home could come to take him home. We never saw him at a meeting again.

Art's Odyssey Unplanned

One of the pleasures of scouting had nothing at all to do with the scouts. It was a walk of several blocks from our house to Carleton School. Pa had been outside all day in all kinds of weather, but he never missed walking with me to a scout meeting. He'd tell me about a lot of things that happened when he was a kid.

Like me, he'd been a sickly and weak kid, but he also had fears that I didn't. Grandma and Grandpa Schmitz were fairly well off and could buy him almost anything he wanted. They offered to buy him a bicycle, but he turned it down.

He told me about how he felt when a friend trying to hitch a ride on a freight train got killed when he fell under the wheels. I also learned why he so enjoyed taking us on our Sunday bumming around town outings. Grandpa'd taken him to places when he was a kid.

The Van Oss family lost their house and moved to an apartment in West Milwaukee. After they got settled, we were invited to lunch on a Sunday afternoon. Even though it took some time to get there by bus and streetcar, lunch wasn't quite ready because Mrs. Van Oss confessed, the first Devil's Food cake she'd made fell, so she felt she had to make another one. Sis and I asked her if we could have a piece of the fallen cake while we waited for the lunch to be ready.

Ma and Mrs. Van Oss said it'd be all right, so Sis and I went into a space near the kitchen where the obviously fallen cake sat on a shelf. We helped ourselves to a piece and it tasted pretty good, so we had another slice that tasted just as good, and before we'd finished, we'd eaten the whole cake.

Ma was pretty upset, and Harold smirked at us getting bawled out, but Mrs. Van Oss said we'd saved her from having to dispose of it. It hadn't affected our appetites for the rest of the roast beef dinner we ate. Their son Adrian was out with friends.

Harold and I were wearing out our shoes so fast Ma started taking us to Browers shoe store downtown. We loved it. With each pair of shoes, that had a shark's skin front on top, we got a shark's tooth! And, to make sure the shoes were big enough, we used a machine in the store that x-rayed our feet with the shoes on. Nobody else at school had done that.

Ma'd grown up in abject poverty and made certain her kids weren't going to suffer the same teasing she'd endured with Grandma's homemade dresses. When I was ten, Harold and I were outfitted with genuine leather, sheep wool lined jackets that we wore the first day of school after Easter vacation.

We didn't know what hit us! A bunch of boys tore into us on the playground at recess, not hurting us physically, but tearing our new jackets apart so the linings could be seen through the rips in the leather. The problem was that the guys were lucky to have any clothes to wear to school, to say nothing of so obviously new jackets. Pa was one of the few fathers that had a paying job. Ma was devastated, we were just glad we hadn't been hurt. Nobody was punished.

Marjorie Kelling was one of the nicer girls in my class. Her father was some kind of wheel in a coal company. I'd seen my share of movies, but I hadn't known there were other kinds of movies not shown in theaters.

Art's Odyssey Unplanned

One morning, we were led to a large assembly room in the basement of the school with no idea of the purpose. Seated on individual wooden chairs, the room was darkened, and on a portable screen set up, I was entranced by a movie showing coal boats being loaded, sailing on the lake, and then with huge conveyor systems, being unloaded at their dock in Milwaukee. This was so much better than having to do stuff in a classroom. We didn't even have to write a report on it.

Once a week we had an art class. The teacher would put something on her desk, and tell us to draw a picture of it. Once there was a beautiful, but complex flower to draw, and then color in.

I knew there was no way I could duplicate on paper the intricacies of the blossom, so I did the next best thing. I drew and colored a picture of a cosmos, a flower Ma grew in her garden.

One Monday we were assigned the work of drawing something from our imagination. That I could do. Pa'd had us at the Rapid Transit depot the day before.

I drew a fairly detailed picture of a Rapid Transit train, including everything I could recall seeing, the light fixture on the front of the first car between the bottom of the car and the windows above. I drew the front of the top, the green of the coach, with the yellow border above the windows and the roof, and just for good measure, the rivets holding a lot of it together. Then I got chastised. My work was a recalled copy of something I'd already seen, not an imaginary subject.

I loved our lake front. One lazy summer afternoon,

Art Schmitz

I'd taken a #21 North Avenue Trolley Bus to the east end of the line. It was only a short walk east, across Lake Drive, past St. Mary's Hospital on the north, and what Pa called the Water Tower on the South.

I guess the Water Tower somehow had been used to get water from the lake to people in the city way back when. Before walking down to the lake, I stopped to take a look at the Water Tower.

There was an open door at the base of the tower, and curiosity got the best of me. Looking inside, I saw that the structure was now being used as a storage place for DPW small equipment. Next to some of the equipment and tools was the base of a spiral staircase.

It took a while, but I was able to climb all the way to the top, ending at a kind of observation area with windows facing in all directions.

I must have spent at least an hour enjoying the views of the city and the lake areas, before gradually making my descent to the base and the still open door. It was a long time after that before I began to think about what I would have done if someone had closed and locked the door before I'd come down.

By our third year at Peninsula I had a little Kodak 127 camera with me. Although Bobby wasn't crazy about heights, he climbed up the observation tower with me one day. From there I got a great look at a steam boat way out on the water. Bobby told me not to try to take a picture of it; it was too far out to show up. I disagreed, and snapped the picture. It took a week after we got back before I could go to Bobby's house and show him a great shot of the boat.

Pa often took us kids on hikes in the woods at

Art's Odyssey Unplanned

Peninsula, and as we grew we went hiking on our own. We often saw porcupines that ignored our presence, but we knew better than to do anything that would result in picking quills out of our hands. There'd also be the occasional deer, and sometimes a skunk.

In 1939, Harold and I seriously planned on riding our bikes to the New York World's Fair. We weren't concerned about the distance, and gave no thought to where we'd stay overnight on the way or when we got there. The same thing with eating.

Ma was worried sick about our intentions and I overheard her one night asking Pa; "You're not going to let them do that, are you?" Pa didn't answer her. But, when it came time to head up to Peninsula, our bikes were strapped to the front and back bumpers of our Chev.

Bobby, of course, was with us, but biking wasn't his thing; too much work. Harold and I explored other areas of the park we'd never thought about before, from the Golf Course on one end of the park to some of the places in Fish Creek of interest to us, like where we could buy malts, sodas, or sundaes. Nobody ever said anything more about biking to New York.

In 1939, the Dominican Republic issued a stamp relating to a proposed new lighthouse with a totally different design shown on the stamp. That stamp suggested an adventure I'd have getting from Miami, Florida to Santo Domingo that didn't look that far away on a map; too far to swim of course, but I figured there must be boats running back and forth. In comparison, getting to Miami would be the easy part.

The last fall days of 1941 were cold and snowy. I had an inner feeling of euphoria writing Christmas cards at the dining room table in a warm house in the evening, watching snowflakes falling outside the window, while listening to Bing Crosby on the radio, singing "I'm Dreaming of a White Christmas."

I was 18 and due to graduate in February of 1942. I'd learned a great way to add to my stamp collection was through correspondence with pen pals in other parts of the world.

I loved the varied and colorful appearance of foreign stamps, most with designs, words, and pictures very different from ours. One of my correspondents was an 18-year-old girl in Tokyo, Japan.

I listened to the radio while answering her letter. She'd enclosed a picture of her brother, a Captain in the Japanese army.

Breaking into the middle of a song, the announcer gave us the word that Pearl Harbor was being bombed by the Japanese Air Force. I stopped writing the letter.

Our normally verbose family ate an extraordinarily quiet lunch. We knew we were at war, with no idea of how that would play out for any of us.

That afternoon we drove over to Bobby's house. As quiet as lunch had been, our arrival triggered a barrage of words from everyone about the war we hadn't declared, but had already begun. Bobby, almost 18, Harold a year younger, and I, all had something to say about our chances of being drafted, or what we'd do to the Japs!

Tante Margaret and her current boyfriend Henry were there. Henry, not crazy about kids anyway, suddenly decided he had a letter he wanted mailed from the main post office downtown, and giving me the keys to his 1927 Hupmobile coupe, sent me, with Harold and Bobby on our way with a hint we could take our time.

The only car I'd ever driven before was our 1936 Chev. The Hupmobile body was twice as far above the ground, so we felt like kings as we cruised above everything else on the road. The tank was near empty when we got back in time for a pork chop supper. We didn't know it wouldn't be long before gasoline and meat would be rationed.

On Monday, December 8th, the atmosphere at school was charged. A lot of my friends had older brothers who hadn't yet been drafted, and knew with certainty it wouldn't be long before a lot of us would be wearing a uniform instead of getting a civilian job or starting freshman year at college.

We were scared stiff! If Japan could pull a surprise attack like this, who knew what could happen next. Our comfortable world had been turned upside down.

That day, for the first time in my four years at the school, the principal, Mr. Weingartner, allowed a radio broadcast, besides the usual announcements to be heard by the student body.

There wasn't a whisper as we listened to President Roosevelt ask Congress for a declaration of war against Japan. The eloquence of his short and simple speech equated well with the famous "Blood, sweat, and tears" speech of Winston Churchill to his beleaguered England, and contrasted sharply with the long, hysterical harangues I'd heard Hitler deliver to his nation.

We were in a state of shock that never left us before we graduated in January of 1942. School became a kind of exercise in scholastic futility. We went through the motions of going to class, reciting, taking final exams, going to basketball games, but our hearts weren't in it, and it showed.

We learned later that we'd been screwed. Mr. Weingartner, under the guise of aiding the war effort, convinced our student leaders that the paper that would have gone into our yearbook was needed for the war effort, and the same thing for class rings. Ours was the only high school in Milwaukee that had those limits.

I wasn't the only one deficient in producing the assigned homework. One of my best friends, normally never missing, would have been valedictorian of our class, but was only allowed to be salutatorian because he'd missed a homework assignment when he'd been ill.

It was toward the end of October 1929 when Ma was called to take a phone call at Berbaums. She left us alone in the house, but not for long. As soon as she got back, she had us put on our coats, and took us with her, walking as fast as she could. She never went outside with us, so we knew something was up.

Turning the corner to walk toward 37th Street on Fairmount, she told us we had to hurry to get to the Citizen's Bank on Villard Avenue. She hadn't counted on some conditioning Pa'd done with us.

Approaching the railroad tracks just south of Villard Avenue, the signal lights were flashing and there was a train heading northwest coming. We knew we had plenty of time to cross the tracks before it got there, but it was kind of a tradition that Pa'd let us have, that we'd always have to wait till the train went by so we could see how many freight cars, or coaches if it was a passenger train. Ma was beside herself because she couldn't get us to move until the fairly short train had passed, and no way was she going to cross the tracks and leave us on the other side.

We had all we could do to keep up with Ma till we got to the bank. We just stood around and waited while Ma did what she'd come there to do.

The walk home was a lot slower. Tante Margaret had phoned and told Ma the banks were failing and closing and she should get her money out while she could.

It turned out that our bank didn't close, but Tante Margaret's did and never re-opened. She was so confident that her bank, a much larger bank wouldn't close, she hadn't followed her own advice.

Going to and from 35th St. school, I'd pass a number of business places with windows facing the street. All of them always had fairly large black and white pictures of current news items from all over the world.

When I realized they were changed each week, I went in and asked the owners if I could have the one from the week before. I didn't know if the pictures were kept, sent back somewhere, or tossed in the trash.

From then on, I became the proud owner of pictures with events often appearing in the news reels at the Ritz.

One of the more interesting couples renting the

front bedroom was Mr. and Mrs. Watts. They were also the oldest people. Originally from the upper social order of Cleveland, Ohio, they'd lost everything when the stock market crashed; leaving them nearly penniless.

We had no idea as to why they wound up in Milwaukee, or how they found our house. They had no car. Mr. Watts was a very dignified man, but kind and gentle. His wife constantly bemoaned their fate, among anything else she could find to gripe about.

She did introduce me to a new word. Meeting Eddy Kaupla the first time, she made some remark about my "tow headed friend."

Mr. Watts was looking forward to closing a business deal when he took the train to Chicago for a few days. While he was gone, Pa asked Mrs. Watts if she'd care to go with us to watch the National Guard do some night time aerial training exercises at one of Milwaukee's southern suburbs. "Are the children also going?" She asked. When Pa said, "Of course." She decided to stay home. I didn't mind.

We got a good spot to park to watch the action in the dark sky. Powerful search lights aimed skyward, spotted low flying aircraft. We sat on the running boards of the car to get a better view.

Mr. Watts returned from Chicago with news that the deal didn't go through, and with a very bad cold. A few days later he went to the hospital, and a few days later died. It didn't take Mrs. Watts long to arrange for his body to be sent back to Cleveland with her. They didn't have much to leave with us, but now I had a typewriter I could use at home.

Approaching my 19th birthday, I was getting tired

of working jobs that looked good at first, or for a time, but didn't seem to have any long-term or future satisfaction for me. One day I went to the Milwaukee Vocational School on 6th and State downtown to see if they could give me some direction. Boy, did they ever!

As a counselor and I talked over various possibilities, he wondered if I'd be interested in a new program that was being offered. He made it clear that, although it was using the school's facility, it was being run by the U.S. Army. It would be known as the JRT program; Junior Radio Training. Those enrolled in the program would learn how to repair radios.

To enroll in the program meant enlisting in the Army Signal Corps. Taking care of the paper work was the easy part. I thought getting Ma and Pa's signatures might be a problem. Ma, ever eager to know her son was going to learn a trade signed, as did Pa, who knew exactly what was involved without any explanation from me.

Once the paper work was in order, the next step was reporting to the Army Induction Center at 342 N. Water Street for the physicals and interviews. That turned out to be a real ego boost for me.

I'd seen naked guys at boy scout camp and the locker room at school, but I'd never seen such a variety of naked men as there were here. I thought I looked pretty good by comparison.

There wasn't time to ask questions, but I had no idea why a medic had to shove his finger up my butt, or ask me to cough with a finger stuck next to my nuts. Part of the exam was the eye thing. By the time I'd finished with all the routines, the Colonel in charge told me I was rejected because of the vision in my right eye.

I was crushed. The following week I was back again, hoping there'd be a different result, or a different officer involved. The result was the same, even though a different officer gave me the word. I figured, "Third times the charm," so I went back the next week.

The vision result was the same, but the same Colonel who'd been there the first time was on duty. "You really wanna get in, don't cha?" he said, adding, "hell, it's your funeral" and signed me in. The plus side was that my Army Service Record showed me as a Non-Combatant, meaning I'd be in, but exempt from combat duty.

At the Induction Center, I met two guys from Wausau, Dale Fluegel and Wesley Koefler. Like lost sheep in the big city, they had no idea of where to stay while in the program. We made them welcome at our house, somehow or other, managing to work out sleeping arrangements with no charge.

Each of them had an older model car, Wesley's was an old Chevy sedan and Dale had an old Ford coupe. With the three of us working the same schedule, we didn't have to rely on Pa or public transportation to get to school and back, no matter which shift we were on.

We began our training at 10 a.m., finishing at 6 p.m. A few weeks later we began at 6 p.m., finishing at 2 a.m., and a few weeks later from 2 a.m. to 10 a.m. None of us had a problem sleeping as our schedule changed.

Art's Odyssey Unplanned

Suddenly I was making more money than a lot of civilian working guys were making. Besides getting the standard army pay of $21 a month for a privates rating, we were getting a subsistence allowance for a place to stay and food. The folks weren't charging us for room or board, so we were able to live high on the hog wherever we were.

Dale had friends and relatives living in Chicago and Wes's family was in Wausau. I'd spend one weekend living it up in Chicago with Dale, usually taking the Milwaukee Road train there and back, and the next weekend with Wes in Wausau.

One weekend Dale and I went to Wausau on a Friday evening. His dad ran a second-hand store, and the family lived in what looked like an old Dutch windmill, a really unique dwelling, but very cozy inside.

The next day Dale, some of his friends and I went squirrel hunting. I'd never been hunting before, and had never fired a gun before.

It turned out to be one of the scariest experiences I'd had till then. Dale and I were ok, but most of the other guys were stewed to the gills, and weren't too careful about where they shot. I managed to fire a few shots toward some tree tops, bur I don't think any of us saw a squirrel.

I realized then that my right eye could be a problem if I had to fire a gun in the army. I cringed with each shot as the empty cartridge ejected past my face because I'd used my left eye to aim and fire.

That Saturday evening, Dale went out with some friends, and I stayed back to play cards with his folks, his sister Mavis, and younger brother Elwood.

I'd brought some chopsticks for them that I'd got at Chinatown in Chicago. I won a bet for two bits that I couldn't eat ice cream with chopsticks.

Dale was pretty well hung over Sunday morning, so I asked him if I could take his car to visit the Thomas's in Wisconsin Rapids. With both cities astride the Wisconsin River, I didn't know which one was the worst for finding one's way around. I managed to locate the Thomas's, but had one doozy of a time finding my way back to the Fluegel's home in Wausau.

Driving back to Milwaukee the next night, we were stopped by a local sheriff. Pointing his weapon, he told us to follow him to the court house and we'd better not try to get out of it, or he'd have the whole department after us.

Reaching the courthouse, we asked him why we'd been stopped, as we hadn't been speeding. He told us there'd been a robbery, and the thieves were driving a car exactly like Dales. It took a few hours before we were finally told we could leave, but it set us back timewise.

It was dawn before Dale pulled over and said "I'm tired. How about you drive the rest of the way?" While he zonked out, I took the wheel and drove. The sun was well up before we got to Jefferson on Highway 16. I didn't realize until we got to Oconomowoc that I'd slept the whole distance between Jefferson and Oconomowoc with Dale peacefully snoozing away in the right front seat.

The next weekend I rode with Wesley to his home in Wausau. His folks had Wesley fairly late in life and looked more like grandparents than Mom and Dad.

Art's Odyssey Unplanned

I'd slept with Harold for most of our lives, and sometimes with Bobby at his place, so had no problem sharing a bed with Wesley. That Saturday evening we went to a dance at the outskirts of a nearby town.
As the new guy on the scene, I had no problem finding girls to dance with. We all had no trouble putting away our share of the beer available. It was well after midnight when some guy took offense at my dancing with his girlfriend, and got physical about it.
About that time, Wesley and I figured we'd better get out of there, doing so just before the local cops got on the scene. It was after 3 a.m. before we rolled into the driveway at Wes's place. His parents were sitting on the back steps crying the blues about their wayward sinner of a son leading others astray.
We all drove to their church that morning - don't ask me how we were able to get up to do that. The preacher wasn't robed or anything, and folks on the chairs could chime in whenever they wished. There was no organ, piano, or other instrument to play with the hymns in the book.
Wesley was a ham radio man with his own transmitter in the attic of his home. We spent time playing huge records he got from the local radio station, acting as disc jockeys between plays, indulging in very uninhibited non-biblical dialogue.
Eventually we began the drive back to Milwaukee. There was no state speed limit, but almost every county had posted limits that usually varied from those of adjacent counties. No way could we afford either the time or the cost of a fine for speeding.
One weekday afternoon, a gray truck pulled up in front of our house. Two burly men in formal business

suits asked if Wes was there when I went to the door. It turned out we'd been heard, and offended listeners as far away as Indianapolis.

Wes didn't have a license to broadcast and would be in serious trouble if he didn't get one pronto! He made a quick trip to Chicago, took the exam, which for him was a cakewalk, and got his license.

As the weather got colder, the folks and I went shopping for a new overcoat for me. I'd only worn it for a couple of weeks when Ma noticed that it didn't look new anymore. On closer inspection, we saw that the label was different; it was someone else's much older coat.

We called the police and they sent a plain clothes detective to the house. He asked all of us a lot of questions, and really offended Dale in the process but that was it.

It was a few weeks later that I noticed my friend Wesley Kobey wearing what had been my new coat. Telling him about our report to the police, he gave back the coat with his apologies for "mistaking it for his old one."

Not long after that, Dale was suddenly transferred to Camp Monmouth, a Signal Corps training facility in New Jersey. I lost touch with Dale, but kept in touch with his family.

The training was a constant source of frustration for me. Much of it involved working out mathematical elements like sines and cosines from oscilloscope readings. I liked working with the oscilloscope, but had no idea of what I was doing with it.

The practical end of things wasn't going much better. A soldered connection I'd made to a super heterodyne radio I'd been assembling, came loose and hit me in the hand. The powerful electric shock caused me to fall backwards, landing on the floor on top of the instructor. I wound up with a hole in the palm of my hand.

Some of the guys'd go to sleep under their work bench. A piece of very wet paper'd be put on their thigh. We'd heat a penny red hot with a soldering iron and place it on the paper. The ensuing steam woke the guy up! In one instance so suddenly, he knocked himself out when his head hit the bottom of the work bench.

That didn't last long. In December of '42, the program was closed and we were sent to Fort Sheridan, Illinois for processing into active duty in the uniformed army. From there we were sent to various other camps for basic and job skill training.

The End

www.ingramcontent.com/pod-product-compliance
Lightning Source LLC
LaVergne TN
LVHW041249080426
835510LV00009B/657